U-0201

Keeping
Resources
Human

A Practical Guide
to Retaining Staff

Declan Browne

BA, BD, PG Dip Hum, H Dip Psych, MA, Occ Psych

Published 2000 by
Onstream Publications Ltd. Cloghroe, Blarney, County Cork. Ireland
Tel/fax 353 (0) 21 4385798 email:info@onstream.ie, website:www.onstream.ie
Layout and cover by Nick @ onstream
Cover photo of Declan Browne by John Sheehan taken at Maryborough House Cork

A CIP record for this book is available from the British Library

Printed in Ireland by Betaprint

The moral right of the author has been asserted

ISBN: 1897685 76 9

Table of Contents

Declan Browne has a wide range of academic training.

Majoring in Philosophy and History from University College Galway in the early eighties, he then achieved an honours degree in Theology from The Jesuits Milltown Institute, Dublin, followed by an honours Post Graduate Diploma in Holistic Development and Leadership.

Next, in order to understand more about the individual and the mind, he completed an honours Higher Diploma in Psychology from UCC and continued with a Masters in Occupational Psychology from UCC. He is presently studying for a PhD in Cultural Diversity.

In 1996 he founded ATO Associates International Ltd, a Management Consultancy focusing on support for CEOs and managers of multi-nationals in designing strategies for staff retention and change management. Based in Cork, with company offices in Waterford, Limerick and Prague, his work takes him throughout Europe and America.

Foreword

When CEOs and senior managers meet their peers at the modern crossroads of the seminar, business lunch or annual dinner, a recurring theme or frustration is: how to get 'good' staff and how to keep them.

The answers of yesteryear do not provide the solutions to-day for many reasons. Unemployment has fallen to new lows so now the job seekers pick and choose their employer and leave without much fuss if not 'satisfied'. The person with skills in global short supply such as in information technology or medical care have truly a global choice and increasingly exercise it. In addition to these consequences of labour supply and demand imbalances there are other societal changes which are creating new expectations within employees: for more use of their talents at work; for a better balance between work, home and leisure; for more flexible hours; for more home based activity using modern PC and communications technology.

All of these changes in the labour market present tough challenges to senior management and to the established practices and conventions in organisations.

While a great deal of company ingenuity has gone into new ways of tapping into job seekers and to recruitment generally, it is astonishing how little systematic attention has been given to the retention of staff once recruited. And if staff retention or loyalty is on the management agenda, the proposed policy response is often superficial or partial - in the absence of any well founded guidelines based on to-day's workplace realities.

Declan Browne's book Keeping Resources Human is right at the cutting edge of contemporary thinking on the core challenge of staff retention. He combines a wide range of academic achievements in the human sciences with the practical experience of his consultancy companies with CEOs and managers of many organisations in Ireland, including multinationals. He outlines the Person Centred Management style required to sustain the commitment of employees and provides a host of practical advice to managers on how to achieve it.

I have seen Declan Browne at first hand in the course of his work with the Collins Mc Nicholas Recruitment and HR Consultancy company and can vouch for the quality of his insights and the positive response of staff to his interventions and recommendations.

Padraic A White
Chairman, Collins Mc Nicholas Recruitment and HR Consultancy
Co-author of "The Making of the Celtic Tiger - the Inside Story "

Introduction

Core issues for all companies in today's increasingly fast-paced work environment are **staff retention, staff harmony** and **continuity of productivity.** All three are inexorably entwined. Given the current industrial climate, employees that are not satisfied in their jobs have choices. Staff disharmony and constant turnover of personnel causes general disruption in the workplace and affects productivity. In the course of the book I will systematically deal with these issues, the way that they manifest themselves in the workplace, how to recognise the warning signs and apply effective methods to combat them.

As economies become more integrated so they increasingly encompass a wide range of cultures. In Ireland the economy is growing so fast that skills shortage is an increasing problem. It is suggested that within the next three years 230,000 people will be needed to meet the skills shortage in Ireland. Where will these people come from - Rumania, Czech Republic, Russia, the Far East?

If this is the case we need to urgently address the importance of building a cultural awareness in order to create harmony, rather than discord, out of this diversity. To retain staff we need to work to understand this diversity and look to their needs so that once trained, employees from different cultural backgrounds will work together and become loyal to the company and the company loyal to them, creating a reciprocal working enthusiasm which benefits both workers and their employers.

The Core issue addressed in this book is Staff Retention. As a starting point I felt it important to take a glance at the future of work and potential challenges associated with it, one of the top challenges being staff retention.

Chapter 1 focuses on a worldwide vision in the workplace and its core challenge - harmonising a diverse workforce, particularly dealing with multi-racial environments.

Chapter 2 continues the global theme of a diverse workforce and staff retention and focuses on two questions associated with staff retention: How can we recruit and select a solid, high performing diverse workforce and how can we keep such a workforce contented and high performing?

I decided in the structure of this book that in order to tackle issues of staff turnover, we needed to tackle the problem of why an individual leaves a company. Is it because of their lack of job satisfaction, commitment to the organisation or lack of motivation? Chapters 3 and 4 focus on a number of theories centred on job satisfaction and commitment. Based on research, I suggest a number of guidelines to protect against dissatisfaction and lack of commitment.

From my work over the last number of years with CEOs and Managers, one issue which seems to flow throughout is the psychological issue of Fear of Success/Failure. People seem to sabotage their own success by working well within their own abilities rather then seeking challenges and moving out of their comfort zones. I wrote this chapter particularly to address this issue of comfort zone which leads to stagnation within management teams. People feel particularly involved and excited when they meet new challenges, expanding their own horizons and goals.

Chapters 6,7,8 and 9 all focus on the type of management that is vital for the future in humanising the workforce and meet the challenge of Staff Retention. I call this management style Person-Centred Management. I focus on traits associated with this new style of management and ways of applying it.

In today's and tomorrow's environments what technology is to hand to support a Person-Centred style? Chapter 10 looks at Electronic Meeting Systems and how they support the organisation and I also explore Accelerated Learning Techniques. Research has proved a 40% increase in learning through this method, so we look at how your organisation can take advantage of this technology.

Many of my clients have asked for a practical guide with tips and techniques to be activated to develop a solid person-centred management style, so the remaining part of this book is devoted to practical tips from both my experience and research the world over.

Chapters 11 to 13 give clear guidelines from creating an effective work environment, developing meetings, dealing with people in confrontational situations and closed mindedness, to how to manage change and the insecurities it generates in employees.

By using these tips and guidelines, you create an environment which is more conducive to greater job satisfaction, motivation and particularly more commitment to the organisation.

The best way to read this book is to go directly to the chapter that is currently your issue and respond swiftly to your company's situation.

Above all, at the heart of all of these chapters lies the fundamental philosophical assumption that all humans need to be respected for themselves and not just for their productivity. This is not happening today; Bottom Line is preached from the mouths of prophets. I believe we need to immediately change our philosophical position from one of profit to one of both profit and respect for the person (employee). I believe the only way forward is to make this paradigm shift to meet the increasing challenge of staff retention in the new millennium.

I encourage you to take up this challenge for the good of your organisation and people.

Happy Reading!

Declan Browne

To Annemarie, who, through her friendship and patience, gave me the support and encouragement I needed to write this book.

To Peter and Christian who constantly help me to keep my feet firmly on the ground.

To Roz, who acted as a catalyst in the publishing of the book with great speed and commitment.

CHAPTER 1

Worldwide Vision in the Workplace

By the end of this chapter you should:

- Appreciate the need to understand cultural diversity

- Understand the difference between Universalist and Particularist Societies

- Understand how human resources must respond to globalisation

Fons.
Trompenaars.
*Riding the Waves
of Culture* (1995)

In developing cultural awareness, the approach developed by Fons Trompenaars (1995) specifies a number of distinct phases which organisations tend to go through. The first is to develop awareness of the nature of cultural differences and generate a desire to reconcile the different perspectives into a new and more effective style of doing business internationally.

Lodge, G.C.
(1995) *Managing
globalisation in
the age of
interdependence*.
San Diego,
CA:Pfeffer;

The next stage in cross-cultural competence is to realise that the differences you see in others are also present, if less developed, within yourself. When you see a Japanese colleague say "yes" to a proposal they oppose and have no intention of implementing, you know that there is a cultural reluctance to say "no" bluntly and appear rude, but you can start to see the logic of the situation and the underlying similarities we share.

*A survey of
multinationals*,
(1993, March 27).
The Economist,
p.6;

The first stage in developing the competencies of working across cultures is always awareness. Without awareness of the nature of the differences between cultures, we tend to measure others against our own cultural standards (the normal way of doing things). An early and sometimes painful lesson is that all cultures have their own, perfectly consistent but different, logics.

"Cross-border
investment is
high" (1993,
September 15)
Chemical week,
p.5;

Culture is a dynamic process for solving human problems. It is dynamic because it changes as circumstances change, and it has evolved in a way that is logical to the people inside that culture to help them solve their regularly occurring problems.

The model developed by Trompenaars builds on this understanding by exploring seven major dimensions on which **cultures differ**. Five of these dimensions relate to **solving problems in human relationships**.

They look at:

1. how different cultures balance the everyday dilemmas of dealing with rules and relationship

2. the individual within the group

3. how status is given and earned

4. how emotions are expressed

5. what is considered private and what public

Hofstede, G. (1980). *Culture's consequences: International differences in work related values.* Beverly Hills, CA: Sage.

A sixth dimension deals with how cultures relate to their environment:

(a) do they seek to control it,

(b) or to accept and adapt it?

The seventh looks at time:

(a) how different cultures relate to time

Ogbanna, E (1993). *Managing organisational culture:Fantasy or reality?* Human resource Management Journal, 3 (2), 42-54;

(b) how they perceive the relative importance and degree of integration of the past, the present and the future

(c) how they organise time within this.

Each dimension is supported by a research database of responses to 22,000 questionnaires completed by people working in international organisations in 53 countries. The questionnaire enables participants to choose how they would respond to everyday dilemmas in life and business, and shows fascinating differences in approaches to fundamental issues around the world.

By using this data to put the choices made by participants in a global perspective and exposing them to completely opposite, and equally logical, views from other cultures, we can make people challenge some of their basic assumptions about life and management.

Management literature and practice is overwhelmingly developed and preached by individuals from the Anglo-Saxon world, and not surprisingly, it is laden with the cultural assumptions of that part of the world. As a result, many of the supposedly 'universal' solutions put forward are irrelevant to a large part of the globe.

Much of the world still runs its organisations on a model of

Carnevale, A.P., &
Stone, S.C.
(1995). *The
American mosaic:
An in-depth
report on the
future of diversity
at work*. New
York: McGraw-Hill.

human relationships that is more akin to the traditional family than the functionally organised, formal, vision-led type of organisation prevalent in the US and north-west Europe.

The cultural assumptions in management practice and processes run deep. As an example, let's look at the simple Human Resources/ Recruitment process with regard to job evaluation. Anglo-Saxon cultures tend to hold what we call a 'universalist' orientation.

Universalist Societies

Janssens, M.
(1995).
*Intercultural
interaction: A
burden on
international
managers?* Journal
of Organisational
Behaviour, 16,
155-167.

Universalist societies are those where the rules and obligations to a wider society are a strong source of moral reference. Often Protestant in Europe, they tend to follow the rules even when friends are involved, and often look for the one best way of dealing fairly and equally with all cases. As a result, they are fond of universal or global solutions, policies and business models, and are nervous about being seen to exercise power in a personal and arbitrary way.

Job-evaluation systems developed in these countries reflect this value. The 'best' are so fair that they are based on a scoring mechanism that you are not allowed to understand (in case you are tempted to influence the result). The system scores your job description and announces a points score that determines your pay level, job size and position in the organisation.

Particularist societies

Particularist societies are those where the particular circumstances are much more important than the rules. The bonds and obligations of relationships are stronger than any abstract rule, and the response to situations may change according to the circumstances and the people involved. Relationships are to be protected, even at the cost of bending or breaking rules. Authority is exercised directly and the decision of the boss is seen as perfectly legitimate.

Managers in these cultures (Latin, Asian, Arab and African) ask: "What does the person who designed this system know about my business?" If they decide someone should be the new director, then the decision is theirs to make. If the manager works in the Italian subsidiary of a US company they may well add: "Don't forget to go to personnel and keep filling in the job form until you get it up to 1,700 points!" It is good to keep head office happy after all, even if it bears no relation to the realities of doing business.

When people have reached a certain level of awareness about the nature of cultural differences, they can begin to appreciate the benefits of another culture's point of view. In training, we often make participants prepare a negotiating position while role-playing a culture very different from their own. It is surprising how well they come to understand and appreciate a point of view that they would never have developed from their own cultural stand point - indeed, it is sometimes hard for them to switch back after the exercise.

Once there is respect for different points of view as equally valid, there can develop a genuine desire to create new ways of working together. So long as individuals only accept the validity of their own view of the world, international working becomes a battle to get the French to follow the systems or to explain again to the Chinese that you are working to a deadline.

With respect for each other's logic, we start to look for ways to reconcile our different views of the world into an entirely new way of working that builds on the best features of each culture. Reconciliation is not compromise - it is creating a rich new synthesis that is more valuable than either of the preceding approaches, not a pale average.

In developing pay for performance systems globally, for example, we quickly run into major cultural differences in whether we should recognise and reward individual or group contributions.

Individualistic cultures, such as those in the US, Britain and Ireland, choose the individual and pay the price of impaired teamwork and the tendency to push for personal objectives even when they damage the team as a whole. Collective cultures, such as that of the Japanese, choose the group and

Earley, PC & Singh, H (1995). *International and intercultural management research:What's next?* Academy of management Journal, 38, 327-340;

DeCieri, H., & Dowling, P.J. (1995). *Cross-cultural issues in organisational behaviour.* In C.L. Cooper & D.M. Rousseau (Eds), Trends in organisational behaviour (Vol.2, pp. 127-145). New York: John Wiley & Sons.;

Cox, T.C., Jr. (1994). *Cultural diversity in organisations*. San Francisco: Berrett-Kohler.

often pay the price in a submerging of individual initiative and creativity.

In developing a global approach, it is tempting to try to choose one or the other; but if you choose one extreme, you lose the benefits of the other. Many companies choose to have separate policies for different regions and develop enormously thick sets of global principles and policies.

Ronen, S (1986) *Comparative multinational management*. New York: Wiley

The real question in seeking to reconcile differences is not how to choose or how to add together the approaches; it is rather how to achieve the one through the other.

If you are operating in an individualistic culture, by all means recognise the individual, but why not do it on the basis of their contribution to the group? In a collective culture, motivate the group, but why not do it on the basis of how well it develops the individuals within it? We can harness the strengths of each culture to support the things they are less good at while pursuing a common goal.

Huntington, SP (1993, summer). *The clash of civilisations*. Goreign Affairs, p 22-49;

Global organisations have an advantage in that they operate in a wonderfully rich environment. They have the whole world to learn from, and nearly every culture has unique solutions to offer. Nearly every major human problem has already been solved somewhere in the world – the trick is to find out where, and transfer the learning quickly to the places still struggling with the same problems.

An understanding of national and corporate cultures and the dynamics involved in managing them is becoming essential in business and career effectiveness. Whether managing cultural differences will be the latest fad or will drive a fundamental change in the way we run our businesses, only time will tell. I hope and believe it will be the latter.

Almost without exception, faced with mature and 'developed' markets, major companies are turning to Eastern Europe and Asia as the source for Human Resources and their future growth. If they fail to find ways to work with these very different cultures, the most significant opportunities of the next 20 years will be lost to them.

The lessons of managing cultural diversity are many and varied, but I would like to inject a word of caution on what is becoming a hot issue. Much of the literature and thinking about issues of diversity carries a strong US legal assumption of 'equality as sameness'. The essence of the US approach has been that everyone is and should be treated the same, and if you do not agree, I will sue you.

In the sense that sameness is the opposite of diversity, this could actually be seen as an anti-diversity approach. I believe there is an evolving European view which says everyone is not the same – and thank goodness for that. It would be a dull world if the Italians behaved like the Irish.

A participant on one of our training programmes said: "Sometimes when I hear my company talk about harmonisation, I think they want us all to play the same note." I am a musician myself, and let me tell you that harmony doesn't mean that; it means that we all play different notes, but together we sound beautiful.

This to me is the essence of diversity, whether from culture, gender, race or age; the freedom to be equally valued for that difference, and the freedom to come together to create something more than any one of us could have done alone.

The issue within the workforce of the future is to hold on to our multi-cultured staff. We go a long way to meet this goal through Cultural Awareness programmes and essentially begin to treat people and their cultures with understanding and respect.

Further reading:

Hampden-Turner Charles *The Seven Cultures of Capitalism*. 1994

Hall Kevan *Effective Cross Cultural Meetings*

Hofstede Geert *Cultural Consequences*

Hofstede Geert *Software of the Mind*

Lewis Richard *When Cultures Collide*

Flower Raymond & Falassi Alessandro *Culture Shock* (series)

Kenna Peggy & Lacy Sondra *Business*

CHAPTER 2

Hire the Right People; Keep the Right People

Recruitment and Selection in a Multicultural Environment.

By reading this chapter you should understand:

- Behavioural criteria for job applicants in a multi-cultured environment

- The tools and techniques used for assessment within a multicultural environment

Assessment and Selection for Success

There is increasing interest in the effective assessment and selection of people from different cultures. This is vital for Ireland to meet its skills shortage issues. Most will be required to work in an international environment, whether as expatriates, individuals or teams on short term assignments, regular business travellers or as people who need to work within a dominant national/corporate culture that is not their own.

The Globalisation of business, the search for the best international talent and the enormous cost of the investment decision represented by an international manager means that many international companies are looking for ways to maximise their chance of success. The number of classical expatriates on three to four year assignments appears to be falling, but this is more than offset by increasing numbers of people with international responsibilities and regular travel.

Given this level of interest it is surprising how little is available to support the assessment process in business.

Approach

My approach to the issue has been to study, make recommendations and offer products and training on the three main aspects of the assessment process and how they interrelate.

- What are the **behavioural criteria** that correlate with International effectiveness?

- What **tools and techniques** can be used to identify these behaviours in an assessment context?

- How can **assessors** be trained to interpret the behaviours they see effectively when they are from different cultures than the people they are observing?

20

Summary of my company's research

2.1 Behavioural Criteria

This is the one area of International Assessment that has been quite widely studied - my company identified nearly 20 major studies. The degree of agreement of the studies were striking, leading us to conclude that either everyone had copied from everyone else or the criteria are relatively straightforward. We suspect there is some truth in both alternatives.

The criteria also seem pretty sensible and not surprisingly and it is difficult to disagree with anything on the list. A summary of the research findings includes that a common assumption seems to be made that the more of the following competencies the better:

- Communication skills

- Tolerance for ambiguity

- Empathy

- Open-mindedness

- Flexibility

- Focus on both task & relationship

- Attitude to learning

- Tolerance for different styles & cultures

- Technical competence

- Ability to succeed in Multiple environments

It is my view that in operating across cultures, the valuable skills are in balancing and reconciling these competencies, not in having extremely large amounts of one or the other.

When we examined the list of competencies we had identified from the research we found that they fell fairly easily into balancing pairs. While communication skills and Attitude to learning & development seemed to fall into the 'the more you have the better' category, the rest can be seen as balancing criteria.

It is clear in operating in a multi-cultural environment for instance that flexibility is good - but if all we do is flex, how do we know when to draw the line, for example where ethical standards differ. It seems therefore that it would be more useful to measure the ability to balance flexibility with integrity, than to look at either of these two in isolation.

Other approaches tend to focus on using internal studies or trained psychologists to identify the criteria for success in a specific company or workgroup. At best these approaches identify what made managers successful in the past (by looking at those who succeeded over the last 15 years or so). At worst they encourage cloning by forcing the search for the few Asians, for example, who can work effectively within a very Irish management group environment.

There may be a case for selecting the first one or two people from a new culture to act as cultural bridges for the company, but in the medium and long term this approach denies the diversity of view and talent that companies seek from geographic expansion.

We consider the criteria identified above as suitable for driving an assessment centre approach to identifying ability to work within a multi-cultural environment.

2.2 Tools & Techniques

Assessment Centre methodology with it's multi-dimensional, multi-method, multi-assessor approach has been demonstrated to offer higher validity than any single assessment tool. We consider the work related nature of the Assessment Centre together with a multi-assessor (ideally multi-cultural assessors) approach to offer the best likelihood of success.

Properly designed assessment centres usually have the following elements:

22

- Clear Criteria

- Evaluation of written information

- Job Simulation exercises i.e. in-basket. This technique uses work remaining from the previous incumbent

- Group Exercises - group discussion etc..

- Aptitude testing

- Individual tasks - Interviews, Presentations

- Group assessment round-up - use of assessment formats and 'objective' evidence.

- Trained Assessors

The use of aptitude/psychometric testing is widespread in Assessment Centres but we do not recommend its use in cross cultural groups for the following reasons:

(a) There is little evidence that personality or psychological profiling works across cultures, even where norms do exist. A recent study using US psychological tests to evaluate Chinese subjects found 65% to be clinically depressed!

(b) Some values-profiling tools such as the Overseas Assignment Index from the US claim to be a good predictor of International success. Most only have validity within their own cultural norms.

(c) Knowledge & ability testing can be useful but only so long as such knowledge & ability is not culturally derived.

(d) Even within a culture, and certainly across cultures, testing should only be used by skilled assessors to identify areas for probing - never as pass:fail criteria.

In order to maximise the chances of success we recommend the tailoring of the design of the Assessment Centre tasks to the specific company environment and experiences. We recommend, as a minimum, a realistic individual work task such as a presentation or in-basket and a group discussion to enable participants to demonstrate a range of behaviours.

2.3 Assessor Training

Even the best assessment centre design cannot be successful without the use of skilled assessors. Across cultures there are problems for assessors in many areas:

- What cultural assumptions do their questions carry?

- How should they interpret answers and observed behaviours from people who do not share their culture or first language?

- How can they assess competence across cultures?

- How can they differentiate between answers that are cultural and answers that reflect ability or personality?

The simplest measure is to ensure a range of assessors, if selecting for a specific culture then a national of that culture should always be present. For an international role, assessment by people from a range of cultures will help identify potential cultural issues.

Very often the opportunity to do this may be limited and, if untrained, these assessors themselves may just bring a different cultural bias instead of a balanced view.

We recommend the training of assessors in cultural awareness. Within the team of assessors a common language and framework for discussing cultural issues is a great advantage. Global integration training should incorporate modules like communication and awareness of different cultures. This in turn should include religion, social, economic circumstances and an appreciation of the different attitude to space, tactility, expectations of life, management styles and psychological makeup. Training programmes should sensitise assessors to these issues and develop appropriate interviewing and evaluation skills.

Conclusion

Improving the effectiveness of International Assessment for use in selection, management development and career planning is at the same time one of the most cost effective methods of improving your company's international pool of talent and also one of the easiest.

The recruitment of international managers and employees is step one. If multinationals decide to recruit 50% Europeans or 50% Mexicans, for instance, from their graduate intake they will normally find ways to meet these targets.

Very often these new managers arrive in an environment that is heavily oriented towards a particular national/corporate culture, usually the historic home base of the company. The host culture usually makes little effort to accommodate to the style of the newcomers who either learn to play by the rules or are not valued and leave.

The development of a truly international or global management cadre depends both on the selection of individuals from a range of cultures, and in developing a corporate culture able to value and reconcile different styles. Either one of these alone is not enough.

CHAPTER 3

Staff Retention - Core Issues of Employee Satisfaction

By the end of this chapter you should understand:

- Theories of job satisfaction
- The consequences of job dissatisfaction
- Job satisfaction and task performance
- How to promote job satisfaction

Herzberg, F.
(1966) . *Work and
the nature of
man*. Cleveland:
World.

Before we find solutions to the problem of staff retention we
must give some time to understanding:

- Why people work at particular jobs and why they leave.

- What makes some people more satisfied with their jobs
  than others?

Hise, P. (1994)
*The motivational
employee
satisfaction
questionnaire.*
Inc., pp. 73-75.

- What underlying processes account for people's feelings
  of job satisfaction?

- Is it always money, or is it a deeper held need to satisfy
  their more personal needs?

Insight into these important questions is provided by various
theories of job satisfaction and are worth studying in order
to choose an effective solution for specific problems.

We will describe three of the most influential approaches -
Herzberg's two- factor theory, Locke's value theory and
Mobley's Voluntary Turnover Model.

Herzberg's Two-Factor Theory

Think about something that may have happened in your job
that made you feel especially satisfied or dissatisfied. What
were these events? Over 30 years ago Frederick Herzberg
posed this question to more than 200 accountants and
engineers and carefully analysed their responses. What he
found was somewhat surprising: different factors accounted
for job satisfaction and dissatisfaction.

Although you might expect that certain factors lead to
satisfaction when they are present and dissatisfaction when
they are absent, this was not the case. Job satisfaction and
dissatisfaction were found to stem from different sources. In
particular, dissatisfaction was associated with conditions
surrounding the jobs (e.g., working conditions, pay, security,
quality of supervision, relations with others) rather than the
work itself. Because these factors can prevent negative
reactions, Herzberg referred to them as hygiene (or

maintenance) factors. By contrast, satisfaction was associated with factors associated with the work itself or to outcomes directly derived from it, such as the nature of their jobs, achievement in the work, promotion opportunities, and chances for personal growth and recognition. Because such factors were associated with high levels of job satisfaction, Herzberg called them motivators.

Concerned, as it is, with both motivators and hygiene factors, Herzberg's theory is referred to as the two-factor theory. Research testing this theory has yielded mixed results. Some studies have found that job satisfaction and dissatisfaction were based on different factors and that these are in-keeping with the distinction made by Herzberg. Other studies, however, have found that factors labelled as hygienes and motivators exerted strong effects on both satisfaction and dissatisfaction, thereby casting doubt on the two-factor theory. In view of such equivocal evidence, we must label Herzberg's theory as an intriguing but unverified framework for understanding job satisfaction.

Still, this theory has important implications for managing organisations. Specifically, managers would be well advised to focus their attention on factors known to promote job satisfaction, such as opportunities for personal growth. Indeed, several of today's companies have realised that satisfaction within their workforces is enhanced when they provide opportunities for their employees to develop their repertoire of professional skills on the job. For example, front-line service workers at Marriott Hotels, known as 'guest services associates,' are hired to perform a variety of tasks, including checking guests in and out, carrying their bags, and so on. Instead of doing just one job, this approach enables Marriott employees to call upon and develop many of their talents, thereby adding to their level of job satisfaction

According to Herzberg's two-factor theory, job satisfaction is caused by a set of factors referred to as motivators, whereas job dissatisfaction is caused by a different set of factors,

Bedian, A.G., Ferris, G. R., & Kacmar, K.M. (1994). *Age, Tenure, and job satisfaction: A tale of two perspectives.* Journal of Vocational Behaviour, 40, 33-48.

Dalton, D.R., & Todor, W.D. (1993) . *Turnover, transfer, absenteeism: An interdependent perspective.* Journal of Management, 19, 193-219.

Quarstein,V.A., McAfee, R.b.,&Glassman, M. (1992). *The situational occurrences theory of Job Satisfaction.* Human relations, 45, 859-873.

Locke,E.A. (1976). *The nature and causes of job satisfaction.* In M.D. Dunnette (Ed.), Handbook of industrial and organisational psychology (pp. 1297-1350) . Chicago: Rand McNally.

known as hygiene factors.

The two-factor theory also implies that steps should be taken to create conditions that help avoid dissatisfaction, and it specifies the kinds of variables required to do so (i.e. hygiene factors). For example, creating pleasant working conditions may be quite helpful in getting people to avoid being dissatisfied with their jobs. Specifically, research has shown that dissatisfaction is great under conditions that are highly overcrowded, dark, noisy, have extreme temperatures, and poor air quality. These factors, associated with the conditions under which work is performed, but not directly linked to the work itself, contribute much to the levels of job dissatisfaction encountered.

Locke's Value Theory.

A second important theory of job satisfaction is Locke's value theory. This conceptualisation claims that job satisfaction exists to the extent that the job outcomes (such as rewards) an individual receives, matches those outcomes that are desired. The more people receive outcomes they value, the more satisfied they will be; the less they receive outcomes they value, the less satisfied they will be. Locke's approach focuses on any outcomes that people value, regardless of what they are. The key to satisfaction in Locke's theory is the discrepancy between those aspects of the job one has and those one wants; the greater the discrepancy, the less people are satisfied.

Recent research provides good support for the value theory. Using a questionnaire, one team of investigators measured how much of various job facets, such as freedom to work one's own way, learning opportunities, promotion opportunities, and pay level-a diverse group of workers wanted, and how much they felt they already had. They also measured how satisfied the respondents were with each of these facets and how important each facet was to them. An interesting trend emerged: those aspects of the job about which respondents experienced the greatest discrepancies were the ones with which they were most dissatisfied, and those with which they experienced the smallest discrepancies were the ones with which they were most satisfied. Interestingly, the researchers also found that this relationship was greater among individuals who placed a high amount of importance on a particular facet of the job. In other words, the more important a particular facet of the job was believed to be, the less satisfied people were when they failed to get as much of this facet as they wanted.

Eichar, D.M., Brady, E.M., & Fortinsky, R.H. (1991). *The job satisfaction of older workers.* Journal of Organisational Behaviour, 12, 609-620.

An interesting implication of the value theory is that it calls attention to the aspects of the job that need to be changed for job satisfaction to result. Specifically, the theory suggests that these aspects might not be the same ones for all people, but any valued aspects of the job about which people perceive serious discrepancies. By emphasising values, Locke's theory suggests that job satisfaction may be derived from many factors. Thus, **an effective way to satisfy employees would be to find out what they want and**, to the extent possible, **give it to them**. Believe it or not, this is sometimes easier said than done. In fact, organisations sometimes go through great pains to find out how to satisfy their employees. With this in mind, a growing number of companies, particularly big ones, have been systematically surveying their employees. For example, FedEx has been so interested in tracking the attitudes of its employees that it has started using a fully automated on-line survey. The company relies on information gained from surveys of its 68,000 U.S.-based employees as the key to identifying sources of dissatisfaction among them.

Consequences of Job Dissatisfaction

People talk a great deal about the importance of building employee satisfaction, assuming that morale is critical to the functioning of organisations. As we will see, although job satisfaction does indeed influence organisations, its impact is not always as strong as one might expect. Thus, we might ask: What are the consequences of job dissatisfaction? The summary will focus on two main variables: employee withdrawal (i.e. absenteeism and turnover) and job performance

Job satisfaction and employee withdrawal.

When employees are dissatisfied with their jobs, they try to find ways of reducing their exposure to them. That is, they stay away from their jobs - behaviour known as employee withdrawal.

Two main forms of employee withdrawal are:
1. absenteeism
2. voluntary turnover

By not showing up to work and/or by quitting to take a new job, people may be expressing their dissatisfaction with their jobs, or attempting to escape from the unpleasant aspects of them they may be experiencing.

Lambert, S.L. (1991). *The combined effect of job and family characteristics on the job satisfaction, job involvement , and intrinsic motivation of men and women workers.* Journal of Organisational behaviour, 12, 341-363.

Locke, E.A. (1984). *Job satisfaction.* In M. Gruenberg & T. Wall (Eds), Social psychology and organisational behaviour (pp. 93-117). London: Wiley.

1. With respect to absenteeism, research has shown that the lower individuals' satisfaction with their jobs, the more likely they are to be absent from work. The strength of this relationship, however, is only modest. The reason is that dissatisfaction with one's job is likely to be just one of many factors influencing people's decisions to report or not report to work. For example, even someone who really dislikes her job may not be absent if she believes her presence is necessary to complete an important project. However, another employee might dislike her job so much that she will 'play hooky' without showing any concern over how the company will be affected.

Thus, although it's not a perfectly reliable reaction to job dissatisfaction, absenteeism is one of its most important consequences.

2. Another costly form of withdrawal related to job satisfaction is voluntary turnover. The lower people's levels of satisfaction with their jobs, the more likely they are to consider resigning and actually to do so. As in the case of absenteeism, this relationship is modest, for similar reasons. Many factors relating to individuals, their jobs, and economic conditions shape decisions to move from one job to another. As you might imagine, there are many more variables involved in making turnover decisions. Many of these are described in a model of the voluntary turnover process described by Organisational Psychologist, Mobley. According to this conceptualisation, job dissatisfaction leads employees to think about the possibility of quitting. This, in turn, leads to the decision to search for another job. Then, if

the search is successful, the individual will develop definite intentions either to quit or to remain on the job. Finally, these intentions are reflected in concrete actions.

Mobley et al's Voluntary Turnover Model

This Model, according to Mobley et al, shows voluntary turnover as a complex process triggered by low levels of job satisfaction. This leads people to think about quitting and then to search for another job. Finally, they form intentions to quit or to remain on their present jobs. At several steps in this process, the probability of finding an acceptable alternative plays a role

Mobley's suggestion that economic conditions, and hence the success of an initial search for alternative jobs, exert a strong impact on voluntary turnover is supported by the findings of an interesting study by Carsten and Spector. These researchers examined the results of a large number of previous studies concerned with turnover. For each, they contacted the people who had conducted the study and determined the precise dates during which their data had been collected. Then, Carsten and Spector obtained data on the unemployment rates prevailing at those times. They predicted that the relationship between job satisfaction and turnover would be stronger at times when unemployment was low than when it was high. When unemployment was low, they reasoned, people would recognise that they have many other job opportunities and would be prone to take one when they are highly dissatisfied with their present jobs. By contrast, conditions of high unemployment would limit alternative job options, leading people to stay with their present jobs despite their dissatisfaction with them. This is precisely what they found: The higher the unemployment rates were, the lower was the correlation between job satisfaction and turnover.

Organisations are highly concerned about withdrawal insofar as it is generally very costly. The expenses involved in selecting and training employees to replace those who have resigned can be considerable. Even unscheduled absences

Weaver, C.N. (1980). *Job satisfaction in the United States in the 1970s.* Journal of Applied Psychology, 65, 364-367.

Gutek, B.A., &
Winter, S.J.
(1992).
*Consistency of job
satisfaction across
situations: Fact or
framing artifact?*
Journal of
Vocational
Behaviour, 41, 61-
78.

can be expensive. With Irish industry facing a manpower shortage, staff retention planning for both the short-term and long-term are of tantamount importance. This book provides employers with the necessary tools to tackle the imminent retention impasse. Although voluntary turnover is a permanent ailment of all industry, some industries suffer more than others. My research in Irish companies has highlighted concerns in industries where flexibility and working conditions have been favourable, yet staff turnover quite high. In these cases, using Person-Centred Management as a tool has ensured employees come on board with the company ideology and feel a committed part of the team.

Job satisfaction and task performance.

Many people believe that "happy workers are productive workers." But, is this really the case? Is job satisfaction, in fact, directly linked to task performance or organisational productivity? Overall, research suggests that the relationship is positive, but not especially strong. In fact, after reviewing hundreds of studies on this topic, researchers found that the mean correlation between job satisfaction and performance is considerably smaller, only .17%. Why does job satisfaction have such a limited relationship to performance? There are at least two explanations:

First, in many work settings, there is little room for large changes in performance. Some jobs are structured so that the people holding them must maintain at least some minimum level of performance just to remain in their jobs. For others, there may be very little leeway for exceeding minimum standards. Thus, the range of possible performance in many jobs is highly restricted. Moreover, for many employees, the rate at which they work is closely linked to the work of others or the speed at which various machines operate. As such, their performance may have such little room to fluctuate that it may not be highly responsive to changes in their attitudes.

Second, job satisfaction and performance may actually not be directly linked. Rather, any apparent relationship between them may stem from the fact that both are related to a third factor: receipt of various rewards. As suggested by Porter and Lawler (1995), the relationship may work as follows: past levels of performance lead to the receipt of both extrinsic rewards (e.g. pay, promotions) and intrinsic rewards (e.g. feelings of accomplishment). If employees judge these to be fair, they may eventually recognise a link between their performance and these outcomes. This, in turn, may have two effects. First, it may encourage high levels of effort, and thus, good performance. Second, it may lead to high levels of job satisfaction. In short, high productivity and high satisfaction may both stem from the same conditions. These two factors, themselves, however, may not be directly linked. For these and other reasons, job satisfaction may not be directly related to performance.

Promoting Job Satisfaction: Some Guidelines

In view of the negative consequences of dissatisfaction just discussed, it makes sense to consider ways of raising satisfaction and preventing dissatisfaction on the job. Although an employee's dissatisfaction might not account for all aspects of his or her performance, it is important to try to promote satisfaction if for no other reason than to make people happy. After all, satisfaction is a desirable end in itself. With this in mind, we now turn to an important question: What can be done to promote job satisfaction? Based on what scientists know about this, we offer several suggestions:

Pay people fairly.

People who believe that their organisations' pay systems are inherently unfair tend to be dissatisfied with their jobs. This applies not only to salary and hourly pay, but also to fringe benefits. In fact, when people are given opportunities to select the fringe benefits they most desire, their job satisfaction tends to rise. This idea is consistent with the value theory. After all, given the opportunity to receive the fringe benefits they most desire, employees may have little or no discrepancies between those they want and those they actually have.

Porter, L.W., & Steers, R.M., (1973). *Organisational work and personal factors in employee turnover and absenteeism*. Psychological Bulletin, 80, 151-176.

Hulin, C.L. (1991). *Adaption, persistence, and commitment in organisations*. In M.D. Dunnette & L. M. Hough (Eds), Handbook of industrial and organisational psychology (2nd ed., Vol. 2, pp. 445-506). Palo Alto, CA: Consulting Psychologists Press.

Improve the quality of supervision.

Machungaws, P.D., & Schmitt, N. (1983). *Work motivation in a developing country.* Journal of Applied Psychology, 68, 31-42.

Satisfaction tends to be highest among those who believe that their supervisors are competent, treat them with respect, and have their best interests in mind. Similarly, job satisfaction is enhanced when employees believe that they have open lines of communication with their superiors.

Decentralise the control of organisational power.

Landy, F.J. (1985) *Psychology of work behaviour* (3rd ed.). Homewood, IL: Dorsey.

Decentralisation is the degree to which the capacity to make decisions resides in several people, as opposed to one or just a handful. When power is decentralised, people are allowed to participate freely in the process of decision-making. This arrangement contributes to their feelings of satisfaction because it leads them to believe that they can have some impact on their organisations. By contrast, when the power to make decisions is concentrated in the hands of just a few, employees are likely to feel powerless and

Page, N.R., & Wiseman, R.L (1993). *Supervisory behaviour and worker satisfaction in the United States, Mexico and Spain.* Journal of Business communication , 30, 161-180.

ineffective, thereby contributing to their feelings of dissatisfaction. The changes in supervision made at the Safeway bakery provides a good illustration of moving from a highly centralised style to a highly de- centralised style. The power to make certain important decisions was shifted into the hands of those who were most affected by them. Because decentralising power gives people greater opportunities to control aspects of the workplace that affect them, it makes it possible for employees to receive the outcomes they most desire, thereby enhancing their satisfaction. This dynamic appears to be at work in many of today's organisations, for example, Waterford Crystal and Aughinish Alumina. High satisfaction in these facilities can be traced in large part to the decentralised nature of decision-making power.

Match people to jobs that are congruent with their interests.

People have many interests, and these are only sometimes satisfied on the job. However, the more people find that they are able to fulfil their interests while on the job, the more satisfied they would be with those jobs. For example, a recent study found that college graduates were more satisfied with their jobs when they were consistent with their college degrees than when they fell outside their fields of interest.

It is, no doubt, with this in mind that career counsellors frequently find it useful to identify people's non-vocational interests. For example, several best practice companies, such as AT&T, IBM, Ford Motor Company, Shell Oil, and Kodak, systematically test and counsel their employees so they can effectively match their skills and interests to those positions to which they are best suited. Some, including Coca Cola, and Disneyland, go so far as to offer individualised counselling to employees so that their personal and professional interests can be identified and matched.

Ideally a company setting up should start with trained assessors who choose employees on the basis of the company's suitability to their needs as well as their suitability to the company. In the long term this makes for a happier, more integrated workforce.

In conclusion, there is good news for managers interested in promoting satisfaction (and avoiding dissatisfaction) among employees. Although it might not always be easy to make a special effort to promote job satisfaction, especially amidst the hectic pace of everyday work, what we know about the benefits of keeping employees satisfied with their jobs suggests that the effort may be extremely worthwhile. Using the techniques described in the book will assist you in this goal and allow you the opportunity to witness these benefits in your organisation.

Staw, B.M., & Ross, J. (1995). *Stability in the midst of change: A dispositional approach to job attitudes*. Journal of Applied Psychology, 70, 56-77.

McGuire, W.J. (1985). *Attitudes and attitude change*. In G. Lindzey & E. Aronson (Eds.) Handbook of social psychology (3rd ed., Vol. 2, pp. 233-346). New York: Random House.

CHAPTER 4

Staff Retention and Organisational Commitment

By the end of this chapter you should understand:

- The Basic Dimensions of Organisational Commitment
- The Consequences of Low Organisational Commitment
- How to enhance Organisational Commitment

Carsten,J.M.,&
Spector, P.E.
(1987).
*Unemployment,
Job satisfaction,
and employee
turnover: A
meta--analytic
test of the
Murchinsky
model.* Journal of
Applied
Psychology, 72,
374-381.

Feelings of Attachment toward Organisations

Suppose you really enjoy the work you do and are very satisfied with your job. This doesn't necessarily mean that you will feel positively toward your company as well. In fact, you may even despise it and hope to get out as soon as possible. Similarly, it's possible for you to think your company is a wonderful place to work, although you might be terribly displeased about the job you do. The point is that to understand people's work-related attitudes fully, you must go beyond the concept of job satisfaction and also consider people's feelings toward their organisations.

Such attitudes, referred to as organisational commitment, reflect the extent to which people identify with, and are involved with, their organisations and are unwilling to leave them. As you might imagine, many factors are responsible for organisational commitment, and the impact of such attitudes may be quite serious. Before you consider the various consequences of organisational commitment and ways to increase commitment, let us take a closer look at its basic dimensions.

Hackett, R.D.,
Boycio, P.,&
Hausdorf, P.A.
(1995). *Further
assessments of
Meyer and Allen's
(1991) three-
component model
of organisational
commitment.*
Journal of applied
psychology, 79,
15-23.

Organisational Commitment: Its Basic Dimensions

To help understand the complex nature of organisational commitment, theorists have broken it down to its basic components. Notably, a distinction has been made between the foci of commitment (the particular entity, such as the group or individual to which a person is committed) and the bases of commitment (the underlying reasons why the commitment occurs). We will discuss each of these basic dimensions.

Foci of commitment.

It is important to note that people can be committed to various entities in their organisations. For example, they may have varying degrees of commitment to their co-workers, subordinates, superiors, customers, the union, or top management - in short, any particular individual of group target. In an attempt to categorise some of these various foci, Becker and Billings distinguished between those whose commitment is concentrated at lower organisational levels, such as one's immediate work group and supervisor, and those who are primarily focused on higher levels, such as top management and the organisation as a whole. By combining high and low levels of each of these they identified the four distinct commitment profiles summarised below.

Becker, T.E., & Billings, R.s (1993). *Profiles of commitment: An empirical test.* Journal of Organisational Behaviour, 14, 177-190.

Individuals who are low in commitment to both their work groups and supervisors as well as low in commitment to top management and the organisation are labelled uncommitted. By contrast, individuals who are high in commitment to both sets of foci are labelled committed. In between are two groups: those who are highly committed to their supervisor and work group but not to top management and the organisation-known as locally committed; and those who are highly committed to top management and the organisation, but not to their supervisor and work group-known as globally committed.

Becker, H.S . (1960). *Notes on the concept of commitment.* American Journal of Sociology, 66, 32-40.

In a study conducted at a large military supply organisation, Becker and Billings found that employees' attitudes differed in ways consistent with their profiles. For example, individuals falling into the uncommitted category (based on their responses to various questionnaire items) were more interested in quitting their jobs and less interested in helping others than those who were in the committed category. Those who were globally committed and locally committed scored in between these two extremes. In conclusion, although this method of distinguishing between various foci of commitment is still new, it appears to hold a great deal of promise as a tool for understanding a key dimension of organisational commitment.

Romzek, B.S. (1989). Personal consequences of employee commitment. Academy of Management Journal, 39, 641-661.

Bases of commitment.

To fully understand the concept of commitment, we must look at not only various foci, but also its bases, that is, the motives that people have for being committed. Historically, two different approaches to understanding these bases have

Tett, R.P., & Meyer, J.P. (1993). *Job satisfaction, organisational commitment, turnover intention, and turnover: Path analyses based on meta-analytic findings.* Personnel Psychology, 46, 259-293.

dominated: the side-bets orientation and the individual-organisational goal congruence orientation.

Becker's side-bets orientation focuses on the accumulated investments an individual stands to lose if he or she leaves the organisation. The idea is that over time, leaving an organisation becomes more costly because people fear losing what they have invested in the organisation and become concerned that they cannot replace these things. For example, people may be unwilling to leave their jobs because they are concerned about being perceived as 'job hoppers' and stake their reputation for stability on remaining in their present jobs (i.e. they make a 'side bet' on some aspect of themselves on continued organisational membership).

Dunham, R.B., Grube, J.A., & Castaneda, M.B. (1994). *Organisational commitment: The utility of an integrative definition.* Journal of Applied Psychology, 79, 370-380.

The individual-organisational goal-congruence orientation focuses on the extent to which people identifying with an organisation have personal goals that are in keeping with those of the organisation. This approach, popularised by Porter et al (1973), reflects people's willingness to accept and work toward attaining organisational goals. It views organisational commitment as the result of three factors:

(1) acceptance of the organisation's goals and values

Randall, D.M. (1990). *The consequences of organisational commitment: A methodological investigation.* Journal of Organisational Behaviour, 11, 361-378.

(2) willingness to help the organisation achieve its goals

(3) the desire to remain within the organisation.

As researchers began to study organisational commitment from each of these two perspectives, it became clear that both approaches were useful for understanding organisational commitment-and that a third was necessary. With this in mind, three distinct bases of organisational commitment have been identified:

continuance commitment,

affective commitment

normative commitments.

Continuance commitment, related to the side-bets approach, refers to the strength of a person's tendency to need to continue working for an organisation because he or she cannot afford to do otherwise. Affective commitment, suggested by the goal congruence approach, refers to the strength of a person's desire to continue working for an organisation because he or she agrees with it and wants to do so. After researching these two forms of commitment it became apparent that a third type also existed: normative commitment. This kind of commitment refers to employees' feelings of obligation to stay with the organisation because of pressures from others.

Questionnaires measuring these three bases of commitment have been developed, and research using them has confirmed that the three different forms are, in fact, distinct from each other. By using questionnaires such as these, scientists have been able to identify people's level of commitment to their organisations and link these to various consequences.

Consequences of Low Organisational Commitment

The prediction that people who feel deeply committed to their organisations will behave differently from those who do not seems reasonable. Despite very complex findings, considerable evidence supports this suggestion. Organisational commitment greatly affects several key aspects of work behaviour.

First, generally speaking, low levels of organisational commitment tend to be associated with high levels of absenteeism and voluntary turnover, in most cases, more committed individuals are less likely to look for new jobs than less committed ones. Interestingly, it appears that people enter jobs with a predisposition toward commitment, and this influences their tendency to stick with their organisations. Lee, Ashford, Walsh, and Mowday (1992) demonstrated this in a survey of dropout rates among cadets in the U.S. Air Force Academy. Specifically, they found that the higher the commitment to the Academy cadets had upon entering

Iaffaldano, M.T., & Murchinsky, P.M. (1985). *Job satisfaction and job performance: A meta-analysis.* Psychological Bulletin, 97, 251-273.

Randall, D.M., Fedor D.P., & Longenecker, C.O. (1990). *The behavioural expression of organisational commitment.* Journal of Vocational Behaviour, 36, 210-224.

Lee, T.W., Ashford, S.J., Walsh, J.P., & Mowday, R.T. (1992). *Commitment propensity, organisational commitment, and voluntary turnover: A longitudinal study of organisational entry processes.* Journal of Management, 18, 15-32.

Mobley, W.H., Horner S.O., & Hollingsworth, A.T. (1978). *An evaluation of precursors of hospital employee turnover.* Journal of Applied Psychology, 63, 408-414.

training, the less likely they were to drop out over the four years it took to receive their degrees.

Second, low organisational commitment is associated with unwillingness to share and make sacrifices. It should not be surprising that these types of voluntary acts are related to commitment inasmuch as we can expect those who are most committed to their organisations to be those who give most generously of themselves. People who are uncommitted to their organisations will certainly have little motivation to go out of their way to do any more than they absolutely must on behalf of the organisation. In fact, they may be out-right selfish and try to get away with doing as little as possible.

Reichers, A.E. (1985). *A review and reconceptualisation of organisational commitment.* Academy of management Review, 10, 465-476.

Finally, low organisational commitment has negative personal consequences. Although one might expect commitment to an organisation to detract from one's personal life (based on the idea that it would be costly in terms of time and emotional investment), research suggests otherwise. In a survey of work attitudes among public employees, it was found that those who were most strongly attached to their organisations enjoyed highly successful careers and pleasant non-work lives. To the extent that work is an important part of people's lives, it makes sense that feeling uncommitted to one's company would contribute to one's feelings of discontent with life in general.

Mathiew, J.E., & Zajoc, D.M. (1990). *A review and meta-analysis of the antecedents, correlates and consequences of commitment.* Psychological Bulletin, 108, 171-194.

Taking all these findings into account, steps designed to generate high levels of organisational commitment among employees seem worthwhile. A committed work force, it appears, is indeed beneficial to both individuals and organisations.

Suggestions for Enhancing Organisational Commitment

Some determinants of organisational commitment fall outside of managers' spheres of control, giving them few opportunities to enhance these feelings. For example, commitment tends to be lower when the economy is such that employment opportunities are plentiful. An abundance of job options will surely lower continuance commitment, and there's not too much a company can do about it. However, although managers cannot control the economy, they can do several things to make employees want to stay working for the company - that is, to enhance affective commitment:

Enrich jobs.

People tend to be highly committed to their organisations to the extent that they have a good chance to take control over the way they do their jobs and are recognised for making important contributions. This approach worked well for the Ford Motor Company. In the early 1980s, Ford confronted a crisis of organisational commitment in the face of budget cuts, layoffs, plant closings, lowered product quality, and other threats. In the words of Ernest J. Savoie, the director of Ford's Employee Development Office:

> "The only solution for Ford, we determined was a total transformation of our company. To accomplish it, we had to earn the commitment of all Ford people. And to acquire that commitment, we had to change the way we managed people"

With this in mind, Ford instituted its Employee Involvement program, a systematic way of involving employees in many aspects of corporate decision-making. They not only got to perform a wide variety of tasks, but also enjoyed considerable autonomy in doing them (e.g. freedom to schedule work and to stop the assembly line if needed). By 1985, Ford employees were more committed to their jobs, so much so, in fact, that the acrimony that usually resulted at contract renewal time had all but vanished. Although employee involvement may not be the cure for all commitment ills, it was clearly highly effective in this case.

Align the interests of the employees with those of the company.

It only makes sense that employees will remain committed to working in organisations when those employees and the company have the same interests in mind-that is, when what

Vancouver, J.B., Milsap, R.E., & Peters, P.A. (1994). *Multilevel analysis of organisational goal congruence.* Journal of Applied Psychology, 79, 666-679.

Caldwell, D.F., Chatman, J.A., & O'Reilly,C.A. (1990). *Building organisational commitment: A multiform study.* Journal of Occupational Psychology, 63, 245-261.

Vandenberg, R.J., & Lance, C.E. (1992). *Examining the causal order of job satisfaction and organisational commitment.* Journal of Management, 18, 153-167.

benefits one also benefits the other. This is certainly the case among companies that use profit-sharing plans (incentive programs in which employees receive bonuses in proportion to the company's profitability). Such plans are often quite effective in enhancing organisational commitment, especially when they are perceived to be administered fairly.

For example, the Holland, Michigan, auto parts manufacturer, Prince Corporation, gives its employees yearly bonuses based on several indices: the company's overall profitability, the employee's unit's profitability, and each individual's performance. Similarly, workers at Allied Plywood Corporation (a wholesaler of building materials in Alexandria, Virginia) receive cash bonuses based on company profits, but these are distributed monthly as well as yearly. The monthly bonuses are the same size for all, whereas the annual bonuses are given in proportion to each employee's individual contributions to total profit, days worked, and performance. These plans are good examples of some of the things companies are doing to enhance commitment. Although the plans differ, their underlying rationale is the same: by letting employees share in the company's profits, they are more likely to see their own interests as consistent with those of their company. When these interests are aligned, commitment is high.

Whitener, E. M., & Waltz, P.M. (1993). *Exchange theory determinants of affective and continuance commitment and turnover.* Journal of Vocational Behaviour, 42, 265-281.

Recruit and select newcomers whose values closely match those of the organisation.

Just as individuals have certain things they value (e.g., preserving the natural environment, respect for law and order), so, too, do organisations. In fact, organisations frequently state their values, in documents known as mission statements (documents in which organisations formally state their basic values and purpose). As you might imagine, the more closely the values of an organisation match the values of the individuals employed in them, the more strongly those employees will be committed to the organisations. For example, someone who finds environmental pollution unacceptable probably would be unwilling to work in a factory that emits hazardous chemicals into the air. Our advice is clear: both organisations and prospective new employees should pay close attention to the extent to which their values closely mesh (such as by carefully reviewing the company's mission statement during the interview process). Failure to do so may lead to a very brief - and potentially unsettling - association.

Recruit carefully

The recruitment process is not only important insofar as it provides opportunities to find people whose values fit those of the organisation, but also because of the dynamics of the recruitment process itself. In this connection, the more an organisation invests in someone by working hard to lure him or her to the company, the more that individual is likely to return the same investment of energy by expressing commitment toward the organisation. In other words, companies that show their employees they care enough to work hard to attract them are likely to find strong commitment among those who are so actively courted.

In conclusion, it is useful to think of organisational commitment as an attitude that may be influenced by managerial actions. **Not only might people be selected who are predisposed to be committed to the organisation, but also various measures can be taken to enhance commitment in the face of indications that it is suffering.** Given the problems associated with having an uncommitted workforce, it would appear wise to consider such efforts carefully.

Meyer, J.P., & Allen, N.J. (1991). *A three-component conceptualisation of organisational commitment.* Human Resource Management Review, 1, 61-89.

Somers, M.J. (1995). *Organisational commitment, turnover and absenteeism* Journal of organisational behaviour, 16, 49-58.

Curry, J.P., Wakefield, D.S., Price, J.L., & Mueller, C.W. (1986). *On the causal ordering of job satisfaction and organisational commitment.* Academy of management Journal, 29, 8467-858

CHAPTER 5

How Fear of Success/Failure affects Staff Retention

By the end of this chapter you should understand:

- What holds us back from being successful
- Self Belief
- Moving outside Comfort Zones
- Positive Mental Attitude

In order to retain staff we must understand them and view them as individuals. We must take time to see what may be holding them back from giving their best to the company. What holds back employees from seeking promotion? What is making them angry and aggressive towards you, their peers and those they manage? What is holding them back from dealing with conflict in the workplace? What is inhibiting their progress within your company and detracting from their job satisfaction?

Thousands of us, it seems, fear success as much as failure. In the eyes of others we are successful already; we are employers, senior employees with responsibility and status. We appear quite normal, we interact quite well, we communicate, we head meetings, and yet we are unhappy, knowing we have not fulfilled our potential. We dread conflict, we are reactive. We blame lack of opportunity, bad luck, bad bosses, bad marks in exams on our lack of happiness, our lack of job satisfaction. So what is the problem, what inhibits us? In working to keep staff we must appreciate the possibilities behind employees reluctance to perform well. Instinctively we know they have potential, yet they under-perform when given opportunities. If we get behind the reasons for this we have the potential to bring employees and even ourselves out from under the rock which weighs heavily on our backs and reveal the hidden potential of the individual.

If we picture the conscious and subconscious parts of the human mind as an iceberg, the conscious mind can be represented as the section above the surface of the ocean, while the subconscious is the much larger part below the surface, approximately 7/8ths of the total.

From birth the brain has 20,000 programmes built in. We know how to breathe and digest at birth - in fact we are born with an insatiable desire for oxygen, food and, perhaps, love. We all have a desire to be loved and accepted.

Working with managing directors and company executives at

all levels of companies in Ireland and overseas I see the inner conflict that success generates. I observe top businesspeople lacking in motivation to enjoy life to the full, enjoy their success. In fact, they play down their assets and achievements.

As children attending our first class at school the desire to be loved and accepted by new friends and teachers is a vital motivator. After a short time in school we begin to be introduced to simple tests like spelling and multiplication which is our first introduction to success and failure. Sooner or later every child gets ten out of ten or full marks for something and, as the teacher returns the marked paper, the child finds that his self-esteem soars for a moment as he thinks about how overjoyed his parents will be, how happy he is himself in his own achievement. Then perhaps that child looks around the classroom, only to discover that some of his close friends did not get full marks, that some may have made many errors. I believe that at this point the child first learns to sabotage - he/she learns to play safe and hide or disguise his own achievement, so that he can continue to be loved and accepted by his friends as well as by his teachers and parents.He/she could possibly begin to connect good events with negative or bad outcomes such as not being loved or cared for when he is not part of the group.

The Socialisation process within Ireland creates in most of us, from an early age, a strong desire to be with the group- to fit in - and not develop one's own Individual Goals. We learn to fear success because it makes us different from others, and we constantly need their love and acceptance. Being recognised is a very basic need. When we move beyond this we want to be accepted within groups and the community. The manifestation of success is always outwards eventually.

I believe that the vast majority of us learn subconsciously to sabotage ourselves so that we can remain safely within our peer group, because if we actually perform better, are happier, more content, then the fear of not being liked takes over and we revert to steering the middle ground rather than reaching higher.

Success means following one's own dreams, working towards becoming contented with life. This is a very practical goal for any person. It requires determination, persistence and dedication. The characteristic of 'not giving up because I believe I can achieve' is a very clear reality in the Dreamer who wants to become the Achiever.

Through my work with many successful managers and sportspeople, one key to success has been that all of these people made an initial decision to achieve a priority goal they set. They realised that living successfully meant living within stretched goals. Goals set the direction and the direction is monitored on a regular basis by focusing on different segments of ones life such as: Career Development, Finance, Family, Social, Spiritual, Health, Attitude and Spouse/partner relationships. One works towards balance when all aspects are reflected upon.

Successful people have the ability to set and work on several goals together. They work towards creating Balance in Life and it is precisely this balance in life, which creates a strong sense of control over one's choices, thus building a solid sense of Self-Concept, Self Belief and Self Efficacy.

It is with this sense of strong self-worth that business people, sports teams etc. can overcome barriers to their success, breaking out of their comfort zones, breaking through their limited belief system about themselves.

It is this strong Positive Mental Attitude that will create the high level performance to achieve their stretch goals.

As I reflect on many case studies of high performers within the business and sport worlds, the key to their success seems to lie in the fundamental principle that your thinking determines all things. If we spend more time thinking in a systematic way about successful outcomes and performance rather than focusing on negative realities, we can then reach the required performance.

There seems to be a number of characteristics associated with the movement towards success:

The ability to move outside comfort zones - to move from known and safe territory towards the unknown. For so many people in Ireland this territory is a move away from our fear of Success and Failure towards a higher expectation set for us through the development of clearly defined, Specific, Measurable and Unachievable Goals. I say Unachievable in that it causes us to stretch and explore what we are truly made of. How often have we heard people suggest that you try to work to your limits. Often we discover that we can achieve different results from that which we thought were possible. This is obvious from achievers in sport and business. We all know of high achievers who broke new barriers in sports results and in innovation. We as humans tend to put limits on our reality by the way we think about ourselves and what we want to become. This limitation is formed usually from past experiences. However **we can change** our view of ourselves. One powerful technique used to help us is Imagery. By focusing on an Unachievable Goal as being achieved and seeing it with one's /mind's eye\ on a daily basis you become more focused on it, thinking of it in a positive manner, thus eventually bringing it into reality. With the imagination, you need to believe that it actually happened.

In order to move from these secure zones we need to have a strong sense of **self-belief**. This positive self-image can be developed and maintained with the use of Positive self-talk statements about the self. This should not be feared as it is an enriching experience.

In order to begin to take control over our destiny through setting goals, it is vital that we have a real, effective **stress management** system. We need energy, adrenaline to put effort into building Positive Mental Attitude in order to move from comfort zones. Today's working environment and lack of balance in life has lead many to enter into Fire Fighting scenarios where very little control is experienced. Very little time is given to the self and the self's life goals. As a response, many are experiencing more and more stress at higher levels so much so that the concept of taking control of one's destiny is a distant luxury. It is vital that a system be found to reduce stress and allow more energy back into the body and mind, to assist in getting back to enjoying life. Evidence has shown that when people enjoy their living, working , games etc., higher performance happens. The secret is getting back to enjoyment.

To move forward towards contentment, happiness, and high performance, we need a personal stress management system to support correct balance in life. The most satisfying experience from this which people tend to acknowledge is that it allows a new energy level to flow. From this it then becomes possible to develop a strong **Positive Mental Attitud**e. It is this PMA which becomes the tool to meet and surpass goals. Imagery has a central part to play in that it helps us visualise future realities we desire and are committed to. Teams, whether Management or sport, all require this strong skill of imaging or visioning the future. This creates the desire, the commitment. Every person need to know what they are moving towards, imagery facilitates this.

Life at its best is a series of challenges. A big enough challenge will bring out strengths and abilities you never knew you had. Take on challenges and you will bring yourself to life. Do not let fear of success or failure stop your progress.

CHAPTER 6

Person-Centred Management

In this chapter we will answer:

- Why do Managers need to focus on the individual?
- What is a Person-Centred Manager?
- What is the difference between the old style Team Leader and a Person-Centred Manager?
- Would you make a good Person-Centred Manager?

For staff retention to be a reality, companies must learn to listen. Respect for the person is at the heart of Person-Centred Management and for it be to effective it must be genuine, not a tool to gain competitive advantage. Meetings must be held in an inclusive, non-threatening environment and later in this book we are addressing the practicalities of running effective meetings and ideas sessions. Managers must lead from the top and be positive influencers, facilitators and must develop good listening skills. They must ensure that there is no gender bias or any form of sexist behaviour used throughout the organisation. These skills are an essential element of a company's armoury.

As a Person-Centred Manager, you help people to communicate and work together. You create a framework for meetings that allows people to tap into each other's creative potential. You provide an invaluable service to your organisation as it changes to meet today's need for new business practices.

Leave old ways of thinking and working together, allow old habits to be released to make way for the new. This is easy to think about, but often not so easy to practise. As a Person-Centred Manager, you will be the catalyst in this process for both yourself and others.

The more you think of management as person-centred, whether formally with a group, or informally in meetings with your colleagues, you will discover that you have strengthened and expanded your own ability to communicate and work with others. Your self-esteem and self-confidence will increase and will be reflected back to you and others in many ways.

They can see:
- That they could use dialogue to accomplish their purpose faster.

- That they shared more ideas and knowledge.

- That their results were of a higher quality because

everyone in the group had equal opportunity to contribute.

- That people in their group with differing viewpoints had their ideas married together.

- That everyone left in agreement and with a common understanding of what had occurred and what was to happen next.

Now, relax and imagine yourself being part of a group like that. Imagine what would be easier to do. Imagine what it would feel like. Imagine what it might do for your group.

Person-Centred Management offer managers and employees alike the opportunity to create an organisational environment where the full contribution of each and every member of the group is allowed, encouraged and supported. In essence, it provides the organisation with a natural capability to tap into the hidden potential of all employees and enables the organisation to create a new culture:

- A culture of employee involvement that encourages people to participate actively and to think creatively.

- A culture of positive management where people are involved in problem solving and decision making.

- A culture of ownership where people see themselves as partners and have a strong sense of responsibility and commitment to their organisation.

- A culture of integrity where trust is built and nurtured through an open and caring flow of information.

In short, **a culture of excellence.**

How do People-Centred Managers contribute to this culture of excellence? Simply put, they help people talk to each other, and more. The *and more* is what the chapters of this book is all about. Come join us on the journey of releasing everyone's hidden potential to create a culture of excellence.

Person-Centred Management: The Basics

What is Person-Centred Management?

It is a way of leading others which takes into consideration the individual's needs and aspirations in the context of long-term benefit to the company.

The function of a good PCM is to keep one's team meeting focused and moving, and to ensure even participation. The manager makes sure these things occur, either by doing it or by monitoring the group and intervening as needed. The Person-Centred Manager is the keeper of the task and does not influence the content or product of the group. The PCM pays attention to the way the group works — the process.

The most important job of a Person-Centred Manager is to protect the *process*. The **process** is *how* the group goes about accomplishing its task. The problem or **content** is *what* it is working on.

In studies comparing the working styles of high performance and low performance groups, the only significant, observable difference was the percentage of time the group members dedicated to the *process* they were involved in. More than 10 percent of the statements made by high performance group members referred to *how* they were going about it:

How should I go about this?

What should I do next?

What do I need to do this?

Should I stop or continue?

Who do I need to talk to?

Less than one percent of the statements made by low performance group members referred to the process. Ninety-nine percent of their focus was on the *content* of the problem itself.

The Person-Centred Manager is the *protector* of the process. His/her tool kit is a set of techniques, knowledge and experience which are applied to protect the process the group is working through. The PCM helps to create the process, adjust it, keep it heading in the right direction and, most importantly, keeps the people attached to it.

The Person-Centred Manager sometimes acts as a resource to the group in the area of data analysis tools and problem solving techniques and must be comfortable with team building techniques and group process in order to assist the group in performing tasks and maintenance roles essential to team building. He or she intervenes to help the group stay focused and build cohesiveness, getting the job done with excellence, while developing the product.

To keep the meeting on track, the Person-Centred Manager must remain aware of the agenda, the time and the flow of work. Person-Centred Management skills are used to ensure total participation. Person-Centred Managers observe group development, noting both task and maintenance roles, and encourage group members to perform them. They handle inappropriate participant behaviours with skill and sensitivity.

Why Do Managers need to focus on the individual?

- To work better, to work smarter, to work faster.

- To get the whole answer.

- To get more people involved.

- To get new ideas, wild ideas, great ideas.

- To foster understanding, support and follow-through.

These are all things that using Person-Centred Management in your work can help you to create. Do you have to use People-Centred Management to get them? To answer that, let's consider two universal maxims:

The measure of the power of a group decision is if the decision lives through its own implementation

People support what they help create.

What brings down a good decision? People. People who do not support it because they do not believe in it or understand it because they are not part of the decision. Most decisions require the support of many people to be implemented. These people occupy positions within and outside of organisations. They live throughout the hierarchy and they come from different functional stove pipes.

If you want to involve these people up front, you take on two problems: one is the diversity of the people and the other is the number of them. When they arrive to help, they bring with them, in addition to their knowledge: their backgrounds, beliefs, organisational culture, technical jargon and personal behaviours. How do you manage the participation of the masses without losing control, not to mention your sanity? Focus on people is the overall management tool kit used to manage the overhead taken on when the size and diversity of working groups is increased.

The type of Person-Centred Manager you select is very important. They need specialised tools, knowledge and talents, just like doctors and mechanics. Person-Centred Management traits within managers may be enough to improve day-to-day meetings and interaction with employees and colleagues, but for specialised sessions, such as strategic planning, you need to invest in a Person-Centred Manager with that speciality. Systems design or product review also requires a Person-Centred Manager with those specialised skills.

For controversial work, the objectivity of an outside Person-Centred Manager is preferred who can be very effective pushing tough issues because the group doesn't suspect a hidden agenda and there is no fear of retribution. When high level participation and management support is a challenge, paying for the service can enhance the perceived value of the session and the importance of attending it. People want to get their money's worth. When you compare the cost of the service with the cost of inadequate participation, you may find the Person-Centred Manager's fees a veritable bargain!

Bringing people together to make a decision as a group has a number of advantages over the individual decision making process:

- A lasting decision or product can be produced much more quickly in a group setting.

- The group product is of a higher quality since it is based on all of the facts and reflects the needs of the whole system it supports.

- Ongoing support to the decision or product is optimal because everyone involved owns it and understands how it came to be.

- **Rework** and renegotiation virtually disappear when all **stakeholders** initially participate.

Effective Person-Centred Management ensures group success because it protects the process of people meeting together. How? A Person-Centred Manager helps people talk to each other. The Person-Centred Manager conducts confidential sessions which create a safe and trusting environment for all participants to work through feelings as well as issues.

Simply put, you have a group and you want that group to perform at the highest level possible. A group must be provided with skills, tools and strategies to do this. Focus on the individual, whether it's a formal role, or a trait exhibited by a group member, provides this necessary element.

What is a Person-Centred Manager?

A Person-Centred Manager is many things:

- A consultant who designs work sessions with a specific focus or intent.

- An advisor to bring out the full potential of working groups.
- A provider of processes, tools and techniques that can get work accomplished quickly and effectively in a group environment.

- A person who keeps a group meeting on track.

- Someone who helps resolve conflict.

- Someone who draws out participation from everyone.

- Someone who organises the work of a group.

- Someone who makes sure that the goals are met.

- Someone who provides structure to the work of a group.

- Someone who protects the work of a group from the overhead of a group.

What a Person-Centred Manager Isn't

There's an interloper afoot in the world of management! This netherworld figure has been spotted lurking near flip chart easels around the globe. You can't spot him from a distance, because he holds the magic marker well and can rip a flip chart sheet clean at the top every time. However, this impostor, this wolf in sheep's clothing, the Manipulator in Person-Centred Manager's clothing, can be detected immediately anywhere near a fresh flow of ideas. Signs to watch and listen for are:

- Changing the wording of a participant.

- Refusing to record an idea (looks tired, got distracted, too many ideas coming at once).

- Getting involved in the content of the group work.

- Fixing the group (even in the most loving way!)

- Fixing the problem for the group.

- Attaching to outcomes.

- Judging comments of the group

- Liking some ideas better than others.

- Flip flopping the agenda and work processes.

- Manipulating people and behaviours through their own feedback.

- Monopolising conversation.

- Taking sides on issues or people.

- Being closed to group suggestions on the process.

- Trying to have all the answers.

Some sub-species of this impostor are quite strong and come and go by their own design, but many of these poor, hapless creatures are created by those around them.

> They are created by becoming Person-Centred Managers without the training and experience they need.

> They are created by being Person-Centred Managers who are not willing to work on their own personal character development every day.

> They are created by overworking a good Person-Centred Manager.

> They are created by being outside of their area of speciality.

> They are created by people pushing them into situations where they are not objective.

All Person-Centred Managers can be temporarily transformed into this lower element by walking into the wrong condition, so it's important for Person-Centred Managers to know enough to turn a session down.

What's the Difference between the old style Team Leader and a Person-Centred Manager?

The responsibilities of a Person-Centred Manager differ from those of a team leader. The highly skilled PCM must have a comprehensive knowledge of group dynamics, group process, and Person-Centred Manager intervention strategies. The PCM is able to handle issues including member conflict, communication obstacles, low performance, leader domination, and group apathy. He or she may walk into a session and have the anger and frustration of all the people in the room directed at — the manager! The Person-Centred Manager is able to handle that, too!

A team leader fills the leader role on the team. They may or may not have actual supervisory duties, but they're perceived to have them because of upper management directive and placement in this role. An empowered team (usually called self-managed or self-directed) will choose the leader and define the expected duties of the person who assumes the leader role.

The Person-Centred Manager's responsibility is to provide a session that will produce products that the team leader needs at this point in the overall mission. The problem being worked and the content of the session is still owned by the team leader.

Typically, the leader has chosen a Person-Centred session so that he or she can participate with the group, playing a peer-level role instead of the management role. Sometimes the team leader will have hired the Person-Centred Manager to encourage a more open exchange of ideas or faster paced, interactive work than is possible on a day-to-day basis.

Would I make a good Person-Centred Manager?

Here are a few questions to help you answer that question. Only you can answer these questions and there's no right or wrong answer, so you can't fail! Your honest answers will help you determine if you would be comfortable as a PCM.

1. Are you willing to listen to others without judgement or preconceived notions about what they should or shouldn't say or do?

2. Do you show respect for the opinions of others even when they disagree with you?

3. Can you release the need to have complete control of a conversation or other situations?

4. Are you comfortable dealing with conflict?

5. Are you comfortable speaking in public?

6. Are you able to laugh at yourself?

7. Can you think on your feet?

8. Do you believe that groups working together are smarter than individuals working alone?

9. Can you accept feedback from others about yourself?

Answering yes to a majority of these questions indicates that you would be comfortable in the role of Person-Centred Manager. All of these traits can be learned and improved and the Person-Centred Management process itself will expand them in you.

If you answered no to any of these questions, do not be discouraged. It means these are the areas in which you will need to change some things about yourself like a belief, an attitude, or an action. Can you change? Of course. Go for it!

Chapter 7

Bringing People Back into the Formula

This chapter will help you to understand

- Group Behaviours

- Role and Description of the Behaviour

- Individual Behaviours

- Cohesiveness: getting the Team Spirit

If you don't believe that groups working together are really smarter than individuals working alone, the 2 + 2 = 5 synergistic equation, I recommend you either change your beliefs or do not enter into the person centred role of management.

In order to tap into the creative potential of each and every group member, you must create synergy in the group. This can't be done without believing in the synergistic principle governing groups. The techniques you use and the style you choose will either help create synergy or block it.

Before we explore people's behaviours in groups, let's take a stroll down the group's development stages.

Stages in the development of groups

Just as infants develop in certain ways during their first months of life, groups also show relatively stable signs of maturation and development. One popular theory identifies five distinct stages through which groups develop.

The first stage of group development is known as FORMING. During this stage, the members get acquainted with each other. They establish the ground rules by trying to find out what behaviours are acceptable, with respect to both the job (how productive they are expected to be) and interpersonal relations (who's really in charge). During the forming stage, people tend to be a bit confused and uncertain about how to act in the group and how beneficial it will be to become a member of the group. Once the individuals come to think of themselves as members of a group, the forming stage is complete.

The second stage of group development is referred to as STORMING. As the name implies, this stage is characterised by a high degree of conflict within the group. Members often resist the control of the group's leaders and show hostility toward each other. If these conflicts are not resolved and group members withdraw, the group may disband. However, as conflicts are resolved and the group's leadership is accepted, the storming stage is complete.

The third stage of group development is known as NORMING. During this stage, the group becomes more cohesive, and identification as a member of the group becomes greater. Close relationships develop, shared feelings become common, and a keen interest in finding mutually agreeable solutions develops. Feelings of camaraderie and shared responsibility for the group's activities are heightened. The norming stage is complete when the members of the group accept a common set of expectations that constitutes an acceptable way of doing things.

The fourth stage is known as PERFORMING. By this stage, questions about group relationships and leadership have been resolved and the group is ready to work. Having fully developed, the group may now devote its energy to getting the job done - the group's good relations and acceptance of the leadership help the group perform well. Recognising that not all groups last forever, the final stage is known as ADJOURNING.

Groups may cease to exist because they have met their goals and are no longer needed (such as an ad hoc group created to raise money for a charity project), in which case the end is abrupt. Other groups may adjourn gradually, as the group disintegrates, either because members leave or because the norms that have developed are no longer effective for the group.

It is important to keep in mind that groups can be in any one stage of development at any given time. Moreover, the amount of time a group may spend in any given stage is highly variable. In fact, research has revealed that the boundaries between the various stages may not be clearly distinct and that several stages may be combined - especially as deadlines and pressure force groups to take action. It is best, then, to think of this five-stage model as a general framework of group formation. Although many of the stages may be followed, the dynamic nature of groups makes it unlikely that they will progress through the various stages in a completely predictable order.

When people come together to do group work without a Person-Centred Manager, their behaviour can be very different than the behaviour they assume under the leadership of a skilled Person-Centred Manager. A skilled Person-Centred Manager will assist them to be the best they can be together.

In making that very positive statement, I suggest you prepare yourself for human behaviour in all of its forms. Learn to love everything about people, even those things you never thought you could. When you do that, you will be able to help anyone you are working with to have the space they need to share their ideas.

Psychologically, the statement "I change the world around me by changing myself" is the key to increasing your own awareness of individual and group potential. If you drop judgement, that change alone alters what you see in your world.

Group Behaviours

Let's begin to talk about people by talking about the roles people need to play in groups. I generally call this **group dynamics**. Your awareness of the roles people need to play in groups can assist you in helping the group achieve success.

When you become familiar with these roles, you will be able to see who's playing what role and if all the roles are being played. If they are not, you, as Person-Centred Manager, can identify the gaps and work with the group to encourage someone to step forward and assume the missing role. At times you may find yourself taking on missing roles. It is to the group's advantage to be made aware of what's missing and learn how to check themselves for any missing roles when the session seems to be dragging. This will allow the group to not only produce the outcomes and products, but to maintain their effectiveness in working as a group.

The roles fall into two categories:

- Task Roles — necessary for task completion.

- Maintenance Roles — necessary for the health or well-being of the team.

Some roles are required for both task completion and team well-being. For the purposes of Person-Centred Manager awareness, We are going to briefly list and explain these roles. I recommend you read, watch subject matter videotapes, and attend training to increase your understanding about group process, human behaviour and team building.

Cartwright, D. (1970). *The nature of group cohesiveness*. In D. Cartwright & A. Zander (Eds.), Group dynamics: research and theory (3rd ed., pp. 91-109). New York: Harper &Row.

Group Behaviours

Encourager: Friendly and responsive to others, offers praise, accepts others' points of view.

Mediator: Mediates differences, relieves tension in conflict situations, gets people to explore their differences.

Compromiser: When his or her own idea is involved in a conflict, he or she offers compromise and tries to maintain group cohesion.

Expressive - Senses the feeling or mood of the group and shares feelings with them.

Gatekeeper: Keeps communication open, suggests ways to share information with others.

Initiator: Proposes tasks or goals, suggests ways to solve problems.

Opinion Giver: Offers information and states beliefs or opinions

Opinion Seeker: Asks for facts, ideas and opinions or suggestions

Elaborator: Interprets ideas or suggestions, clears up confusion, gives examples.

Co-ordinator: Pulls together related suggestions, offers conclusions for the group to accept or reject.

Diagnostician: Helps the group to identify where problems are occurring.

Standard Setter: Helps the group define standards, what's expected, what's acceptable.

Follower: Goes along with whatever is being proposed, agreeable to what the group wants.

Please think about these roles and their importance. Imagine a group meeting where all the roles have been played except for the role of Co-ordinator.

How would that affect the meeting?

What would you, as the Person-Centred Manager, do?

Imagine a group meeting where all the roles have been played except for the role of Diagnostician.

How would that affect the meeting?

What would you, as the Person-Centred Manager, do?

Imagine a group meeting where no roles were being played except for the role of Follower

How would that affect the meeting?

What would you, as the Person-Centred Manager, do?

Individual Behaviours

The most challenging problems in our lives generally involve our relationships to other individuals. When interacting with challenging or difficult people, a tactful approach that maintains individual self esteem wins greater respect and results.

To maintain the self esteem of each individual (and yourself), do not allow an attack on any individual or yourself. Emotional conflict shifts a person's concern from problem solving to defending their position. As the Person-Centred Manager, you shift the focus back to the issue the group is working on. Emphasise that the session's purpose is to produce the best group solution. This reflects what's acceptable, workable, and meets the needs of the group, not the needs of a single individual.

Shaw, M.E. (1981). *Group dynamics: The dynamics of small group behaviour* (3rd ed.). New York: McGraw-Hill.

When you are faced with dysfunctional behaviour in a session, it may be handled by you in two ways: direct confrontation in the meeting or off-line with the individual. The I technique and the F technique allow feelings to be stated. No one can attack another for his or her feelings.

The **I technique** is very simple. Here is what you say:

When you...

I feel...

I would like...

Because...

The **3F technique** is very similar and just as simple. Here is what you say:

I understand how you feel,

I have felt that way before,

Here's what I've found...

You will discover that the group can also be a source of help to you and to each other. I generally refer to this behaviour as peer pressure. When one person's behaviour begins to become disruptive, often someone in the group will take on the role of mediator, diagnostician or another appropriate role and attempt to solve the disrupter's problem or identify the cause of the behaviour.

There is a variety of problem behaviours that can be

detrimental to the group members and their work. I will describe some common types, by their behaviour, and follow them with strategies to deal with that behaviour.

The Know-It-All

This person appears as the expert, wants constant attention and often argues with people.

Strategies include:

- Be well prepared for the topic under discussion.

- Listen and paraphrase what they say.

- Do not challenge — ask questions to lead them to see their errors.

- Praise their ability.

- Focus on solutions.

- Ask other group members to comment on what they heard, redirecting focus away from the Know-It-All.

- Have them summarise their thoughts and record them.

The Sniper

This person attacks and criticises, usually indirectly, masking their aggression by using humour or saying things under their breath.

Strategies include:

- Address the behaviour openly, asking them why they said that.

- Ask others if they agree with the criticism.

- Do not let them hide behind humour.

- Address sniping each time it occurs, until it stops.

The Talker

This person distracts by holding side conversations.
Strategies include:

- Say, "There are little meetings going on. May I have just one meeting?"

- Ask the person directly to share their thoughts with everyone (use tact and diplomacy).

The Quiet Type

This person is quiet or timid. Their silence is often mistaken for agreement.

Strategies include:

- Address them by name and ask them to share their thoughts. Focus your attention directly on them to create the time and space they need to answer.

- Commend their participation when it occurs.

- Talk to them before the session, casually, to help them become comfortable.

- Ask them some safe things early in the session to get them involved.

The Complainer/Whiner

This person tries to put you on the spot to fix it. He or she blames others and never self.

Strategies include:

- Do not be defensive.

- Listen and acknowledge, do not argue.

- Ask questions.

- Solicit solutions from them.

- Encourage them to act.

Long, S. (1984). *Early integration in groups: "A group to join and a group to create."* Human Relations, 37, 311-322.

The Bulldozer

This person will try to run over you and everyone else too! it is their method of stopping progress, because progress scares them. If they can't change, they may leave. At a Person-Centred Management session, bulldozers may leave the room a lot and will have a host of legitimate reasons for doing so!

Strategies include:

- Stand up to them in a non-combative way.

- Do not argue with them. Present the facts.

- Get them into problem solving mode.

- Protect the space of those they bulldoze, by asking the bulldozed to repeat their thought or by asking others in the group how they feel.

Hair-splitting

This person wants absolute answers and definitions.

Strategies include:

- Acknowledge their need for absolute answers and definitions.

- State what you are prepared to give.

- Ask them to honour your work or style preferences just as you accept theirs.

The Interrupter

This person interrupts the person speaking.

Strategies include:

- Say "You interrupted me. Please let me finish my thoughts."

- Whenever they do it, repeat the preceding statement.

The Staller

This person tells irrelevant stories or experiences. They do not focus and instead give off base types of examples.

Forsyth, D.R. (1992) *An introduction to group dynamics*, (2nd ed.). Monterey, CA : Brooks/Cole.

Strategies include:

• Ask them how what they said relates

• Help them to be honest.

• Try to find out their hidden concerns.

• Record their idea on The Hangar (see page 160).

The Inarticulate Person

This person has ideas, but has problems putting the ideas into words.

Strategies include:

• Encourage them to speak.

• Exhibit patience when they speak.

• Ask them for permission to help them phrase or rephrase.

Now you have some knowledge about challenging people and strategies to deal with them. What do you do with the ideal person?

The Ideal Person

This person has good ideas and expresses them freely at appropriate times. They're congenial. They work well with others. They smile and laugh easily, even at themselves.

Strategies include:

• Acknowledge them frequently

• Always learn from them

Facilitating Typical Meeting Situations

Exercise : Please think about the following:

> You are the Person-Centred Manager for this session. How do you handle:
>
> 1. Latecomers.
>
> 2. Inappropriate comments directed at you or at other group members.
>
> 3. Participants not talking.
>
> 4. People who derail the subject being discussed.
>
> 5. People talking to each other instead of the group.
>
> 6. People monopolising discussion.
>
> 7. Sexist comments.
>
> 8. The company changing an agenda item on the spot.
>
> 9. An uncomfortable room (too hot/cold/noisy/etc.)
>
> 10. A person vying with you for control.
>
> 11. The Devil's Advocate type.
>
> 12. The Doom and Gloom type.
>
> 13. The Show Off type.
>
> 14. The Non-stop-Talker.

Cohesiveness: Getting the Team Spirit

One obvious determinant of any group's structure is its Cohesiveness, ie the strength of group members' desires to remain part of their group. Highly cohesive work groups are ones in which the members are attracted to each other, accept the group's goals, and help work toward meeting them. In very incohesive groups, the members dislike each other and may even work at cross-purposes. In essence, cohesiveness refers to a 'we' feeling, an 'esprit de corps', a sense of belonging to a group.

Several important factors have been shown to influence the extent to which group members tend to 'stick together'. One such factor involves the severity of initiation into the group. Research has shown that the greater the difficulty people overcome to become a member of a group, the more cohesive the group will be. To understand this, consider how highly cohesive certain groups may be that you have worked hard to join. Was it particularly difficult to 'make the cut' on your sports team? The rigorous requirements for gaining entry into elite groups, such as the most prestigious medical schools and military training schools, may well be responsible for the high degree of camaraderie found in such groups.

'Passing the test' tends to keep individuals together and separates them from those who are unwilling or unable to 'pay the price' of admission.

Group cohesion also tends to be strengthened under conditions of high external threat or competition. When workers face a 'common enemy', they tend to draw together. Such cohesion not only makes workers feel safer and better protected, but also aids them by encouraging them to work closely together and to co-ordinate their efforts toward the common enemy. Under such conditions, petty disagreements that may have caused dissension within groups tend to be put aside so that a co-ordinated attack on the enemy can be mobilised.

Research has also shown that the cohesiveness of groups is established by several additional factors. For one, cohesiveness generally tends to be greater, the more time group members spend together. Obviously, limited interaction cannot help but interfere with opportunities to develop bonds between group members. Similarly, cohesiveness tends to be greater in smaller groups. Generally speaking, groups that are too large make it difficult for members to interact and, therefore, for cohesiveness to reach a high level.

Finally, because 'nothing succeeds like success', groups with a history of success tend to be highly cohesive. It is often said that everyone loves a winner, and the success of a group tends to help unite its members as they rally around their success. For this reason, employees tend to be loyal to successful companies.

CHAPTER 8

Traits of
Genuine Person-Centred Managers

In this chapter you will learn

What Internal Conditions are required for the effective Person-Centred Manager and how to enhance those you have

Anyone who has participated in more than one Person-Centred session can tell you, all Person-Centred Managers are not alike!

What distinguishes one Person-Centred Manager from another: the bright from the dreary, the energetic from the weary, those who have it from those who don't?

Carl Rogers
*On Becoming
a Person*
1995

Sometimes a Person-Centred Manager can be very effective with one group and 'bat zero' with another. Is it chemistry? Personal style? A matter of trust, background, knowledge, credentials?

All of these come into play between a Person-Centred Manager and the group they're working with. Even though these elements are subtle and hard to define, they're still powerful contributors to the success or failure of a session. I can't measure them and I can't make definitive rules about them, but since they will affect you, let's at least examine them.

Internal Conditions

It is internally that the real traits of excellence lie.

In addition to specialised skills, successful Person-Centred Managers generally have the following traits:

- Flexible ego

- Confidence

- Patience

- Objectivity

- Ability to think on one's feet

- Active listening

- Ability to confront

- Active intuition

- Responsiveness

- Sense of humour

- Articulate

- Ability to summarise

- Flexibility

- Ability to read a group and individuals

These traits may be inborn, and a person who didn't receive many of them probably won't adopt a person orientated leadership style, but I believe that all of these traits lie dormant in each of us and that they can be enlivened. I also believe that these traits can be expanded in any of us whose natural level is already high. Because these are traits of successful Person-Centred Managers, let's play with the ideas of what might be below them and how they might be brought to an even greater power.

Flexible Ego

If you do not want a bruised ego, leave it on the doorstep when you enter the session. Egos tell you what to do, so they're great for keeping you safe crossing the street to get to the Person-Centred Management session, but once there, ask your ego to please be quiet and be your partner because you want to be open to new truths so the two of you can get smarter together. You are not your ego. Your ego is that voice in your head that says, "This is how I'm going to do it because I know best." That's your ego talking; not you. All of the traits have their roots in a flexible ego, that is, the ability to put oneself on hold in order to accomplish a higher good.

Confidence

To be confident you must know what you are doing. Do you have the training and experience you need?
To be confident you must be supported. Do you have the tools,

information and help you require?

To be confident you must believe in what you are doing. Do you enjoy using a person-orientated management style? Do you believe it contributes to others? Do you really believe in the intelligence and capability of the groups you work with?

To be confident you must recognise your successes. Do you give yourself credit for what is good about you? Do you take time to recognise things when you accomplish them? Is your inner critic working overtime?

Patience

"You really have to be patient to be a Person-Centred Manager, don't you?" one of our clients asked recently as I was recovering from a particularly long drawn out rehash of a simmering problem in the group. The immediate answer was, "Boy and how!"

Later, thinking about it, I decided that patience is very misunderstood. It is thought of as something you either have or you don't have — you're either a patient person or you are not. But if this is so, how can Person-Centred Managers be patient in session and then become impatient in a traffic jam later that day?

Patience seems related to your ability to allow things to be as they are and impatience arises when you are concerned with how something is being done: how fast, how well, how neatly, how much like you would do it.

Patience can be learned and improved. You may choose to acquire patience by recognising and controlling what creates it. What you do to control it is to release your need to control everything, all the time. Your daily life is your classroom if you choose to improve your ability to release this aspect of yourself. Open yourself up to becoming aware of impatience as it arises and then practise releasing the need to control the situation you find yourself in. A simple way to release control is to just say in your mind "I release the need to control this situation. I allow this situation to be what it is all by itself". I guarantee that you will begin to see changes in yourself, and the outside world, a few weeks after you begin doing this.

As a Person-Centred Manager, patience arises from:

- Seeing the long-term value beyond the current situation or product.

- Seeing the value of what is being said beyond who is saying it.

- Knowing that the fact that the group is making the decision is more important than speed.

- Knowing that the fact that the group is making the decision is more important than the actual quality of the decision.

- Not needing to be right all of the time.

- Trusting the process, knowing that working through is necessary.

- Believing in the capability of the group.

Objectivity

Objectivity: Uninfluenced by emotion, surmise, or personal opinion.

Webster's II

Even if you are from outside the group, you can still get embroiled in their content if you are not careful. You must maintain a unique balance of being in the content enough to understand the work, yet not so much that you identify with it. As soon as you identify with the content, or personalise it, you are subject to influence by emotion and personal opinion.

A good way to maintain your objectivity is to stay focused on your role and responsibility to the group, which is to protect the process. Remember that your measure of success for the session is different from anyone else's in the room. Be on the look out for:

- Needing too much personal approval from the group.

85

- Answering content questions.

- Caring which way issues are decided.

Ability to Think on One's Feet

You can't think on your feet if you do not know what you are talking about, so for starters, be sure that you are qualified in the subject matter of the session.

You can also enhance this skill by seeking opportunities to teach, give presentations (the more controversial the better), or join groups that will give you the opportunity to do public speaking. You might ask friends or co-workers to role-play with you. Ask them to interrupt, question your statements and exhibit other disruptive behaviours. Role-playing is a safe and non-threatening way to practice thinking on your feet.

Active Listener

I have noted and decided that I have never met anyone who was born with this ability. Listening is definitely a learned skill. It is also a skill that can rust if you do not use it. It is a must-learn for a Person-Centred Manager. There is a number of books and courses that include instructions on becoming an active listener.

Ability to Confront

Yes, you can learn this one. I think the secret is to change your view of what it means. Many of us were raised to believe that if you confront you are being rude, aggressive, and negative. Confrontation can be an act of kindness if you use it at the right time. In Person-Centred Management sessions, you would only confront someone if their behaviour was hurting the group. That's your job. It can be done in a reasonable and gentle way.

Active Intuition

This one can be learned and improved. The key to activating your intuition to the level of being able to rely on it is very simple. All you have to do is trust it.

You are already receiving intuitive information of the highest quality. Everyone is. I know from cognitive science that some people rely heavily on their intuitive side and they are just as effective and right as those who rely on their logic. For some reason, some people's circuitry picks up the intuitive current more readily.

The way to make your intuitive circuitry more receptive is to exercise it. You exercise it by listening to and acting on the signals you are getting. Practise allowing these signals the same validity that you do logical facts, even if you have to kid yourself at first! Intuition doesn't care, she's there anyway!

Start small. The next time you get a flash of insight, do not talk yourself out of its validity. Accept the possibility that it is true and see what happens. The next time you get a gut reaction, follow it instead of rejecting it. If you know who's calling when the phone rings, pick it up and say "Hello, (name of person)". What's the worst thing that could happen? Intuition is like electricity, the current is always there, but you have to plug in if you want to use it.

Sense of Humour

I don't know if people can learn to be stand up comedians, but I do know that people can learn to laugh at themselves. Like the rest of these soft arts, the first step in learning them is to open yourself up to the experience. Put some focus on the matter. Say something like, "Today I'm going to take one opportunity where I would normally get mad and instead I'm just going to laugh". Then do it.

Do what you would do if you wanted to learn how to drop a transmission. Find someone who knows how and ask them how they do it. Come to think of it, if you can find someone who has dropped a transmission or two, they can probably teach you something about laughing at yourself.

Articulate

Yes, you can learn to be more articulate. Public speaking

classes are one good tool. It is also important to be well-read in areas you manage.

Ability to Summarise

Classes in technical writing or journalism can add to your ability to get to the point. So can working with someone who has these skills.

Ability to Read the Group Through Non-Verbal Clues and Energy-Sensing

Active intuition is critical here. I don't think you can substitute intuition with facts, but you can add facts to increase your skills. Books or classes in body language and psychology can increase your ability to sense what is going on.

Flexibility

Learn to be able to be prepared to move away from a plan if the session would benefit. Use lateral-thinking puzzles and crosswords to use the brain in different ways. You need to be able to think on your feet and this requires an ability to change quickly from one train of thought to another.

Responsiveness

The ability to respond to requests of groups and individuals is important. If you are seen to appreciate viewpoints and respond with sympathy you will keep the confidence of the group. This does not mean going completely off track and not sticking to the agenda, but allowing time to consider their viewpoint.

Outward Conditions

For every Person-Centred Manager there are conditions or groups where their effectiveness will be limited. This isn't an indication that you are not qualified to manage in a person-centred style, it just means that you should consider some things before agreeing to step into any situation. Here are some considerations I use:

An outside Person-Centred Manager is usually best.

Because a Person-Centred Manager must remain objective, neutral and fair, it can be very difficult to manage a formal session within your organisation. There are simply too many pre-conceived notions about who people are, how they're going to act, and what they're up to - in both directions. For small, simple sessions your gift will be appreciated, even on your home turf, but think carefully about accepting a large internal assignment.

Have you earned the right to be there?

Most groups are parochial to an extent. For some groups, trust is only extended to those from their own ranks. This could mean a certain background, rank, age, or set of credentials. Both the group and the Person-Centred Manager are better off with a match (even though I know you'd love to help get rid of that kind of behaviour!). Could you be stepping into a condition like this?

Do you have the knowledge and experience?

Some sessions require highly specialised knowledge and extensive experience to do justice to the task. Are you the right person for the job?

CHAPTER 9

Applying Effective Leadership Skills to Business Processes

In this chapter you will learn

The activities which are of benefit
in meetings and discussions and how to enhance
them

Any time it takes more than one person to make a decision, is a time to consider the benefits of a Person-Centred Management style.

Here is a partial listing of different types of activities which will be of benefit in sessions:

- Visioning

- Problem Solving

- Structured Methods

- Open Discussion

- Conflict Resolution

- Subject Matter Expert Brainstorming

- Focus Groups

- Instruction

- Transitions (Reinventing The Organisation)

- Team Building

- Strategic Planning

- Process Improvement

- Data Modelling

- Process Modelling

- Product Review

Basic Person-Centred Management session steps apply to the design and conduct of these business meetings. However, the techniques you will use will vary according to the session type.

Guided visualisation is a technique that works very well to set the stage for visioning. It suspends 'mind chatter' and gives the participants quiet time in their minds to imagine their organisation in the future. After the visualisation is finished, you will notice a distinct change in how some of the participants act and how the group relates to each other. It has a very calming effect.

In vision development, participants are broken out into smaller groups to create their proposed vision. This allows small groups of people to become highly creative together. The individual groups are brought back together and the process of creating one shared vision begins.

A Visioning Session

Creating a vision for an organisation is highly creative. While it requires participants to have experience and knowledge about their organisation and business trends, visioning itself requires imagination. Visioning is asking participants to see the future, to see the invisible. Visioning requires people to suspend reliance on logic and rational thinking and to imagine and then create a desired future state for their organisation.

For you to manage a visioning session, you must have a thorough understanding of strategic planning: what a vision is, why a vision is important for an organisation, how to get a group to develop a vision, and specific examples of organisations that have already developed a vision.

Managing a visioning session requires emphasis on techniques that can move the participants into right brain activity (creativity and images), rather than left brain activity (logic and words). To vision, they need to be taken to a space where the rules of reality change long enough to allow new patterns to form. It is very important to design a playful, relaxed and comfortable environment for a visioning session. This will reduce the amount of time it will take you to engage their right brains.

You begin a visioning session the same way you begin other sessions. This means you will begin in left brain mode as you get acquainted, develop group norms, etc. You then need to establish a right brain connection for the creative work of visioning.

You will want to spend some time educating the group members about a vision. Most people do not know the advantages of having an organisational vision. To discuss available knowledge about what a vision is and how to create a vision, your choice of words is very important. Use words like 'see' and 'feel' and 'imagine' to create images which will connect them to their creative side. you will be giving them words, which engage the left brain, but at the same time, the words carry images to open and engage the right brain.

You may choose to use an inspiring videotape on visioning. You may also choose to take the group on a guided visualisation which allows them to do breathing techniques to quiet their thoughts and move them into their right brain, creative space.

If you decide to do a guided visualisation, you must prepare it in advance and practise doing it. Timing and the words you use to help them create images in their minds must be carefully chosen. I often write down our words, because as you are taking them out, you may go too! The words on paper help keep you anchored to the ground. The Person-Centred Manager needs a little more left brain centring to keep the group on track than the participants do for visioning.

Guided visualisation is a technique that works very well to set the stage for visioning. It suspends 'mind chatter' and gives the participants quiet time in their minds to imagine their organisation in the future. After the visualisation is finished, you will notice a distinct change in how some of the participants act and how the group relates to each other. It has a very calming effect.

In vision development, participants are broken out into smaller groups to create their proposed vision. This allows small groups of people to become highly creative together. The individual groups are brought back together and the process of creating one shared vision begins.

Example of a visioning session

Close your eyes. Relax your body by clenching and relaxing toes first, then each part of the body in turn. Allow 5-10 minutes for this. Breathe deeply as in autogenic relaxation and picture yourself in a dark place, where you feel safe and secure. See a mirror in the room and step inside it. Activate all your senses and picture yourself in a meadow, and consciously try to sense your environment - what do you smell, see, feel? Then imagine yourself flying above your organisation in two years time. How would you like your organisation to look? What size is the organisation? What products or services do you deliver? What's the general mood of your employees working in the organisation? Do they seem contented, do you seem to have a lot of Industrial Relations problems? And in general what is the overall atmosphere, does it seem to be stale or does it seem to be progressive, innovative, or depressive? Are the employees smiling? What significant images come to mind? Come out of the meadow and the mirror and open your eyes and write down what you saw. You may have seen symbols or images associated with where you want your company to be. Are they the same as your colleagues who were visioning at the same time? Once all images are described after the exercise, the group looks at common images they would like to see. This formulates a common vision.

When people create an image they feel part of the company, part of the creative process and it helps them to feel a worthwhile part of an important entity.

The Constructive Response and the Go Around techniques (see chapter 13) work very well for examining each vision. List what people like and what concerns them about each proposed vision. Once that's done, you have a list of the things the group likes and usually they are able to take these things and develop the vision from them.

To end your portion of the visioning session, congratulate the group on their new vision. Turn the session over to your colleague as he or she will wish to talk further to the participants about the vision.

Systems Development Sessions

Systems developers and the business managers they support have discovered that using person-centred sessions instead of one-on-one analysis techniques can speed up steps in the development process from thirty to seventy-five percent. The quality of the products increases also because the users become active partners in development.

In the systems development world these sessions are often called **Joint Application Design,** (JAD) sessions. They are a key element of a modern development style called Rapid Application Development, or RAD. RAD is exactly what it sounds like, Rapid Development. The theory behind RAD is that new systems should be fielded in modules, no working module taking more than 3 months to deliver. This keeps the requesting user engaged and interested because they see results.

To achieve RAD, much of the communication between the technical developers and the user community takes place in a managed session environment. These sessions are conducted for:

- Identifying systems requirements

- Process modelling

- Data modelling

- Planning

- System design activities

- Prototyping

- Testing

• Reviews

To manage such sessions you must have technical knowledge of the methodology being used, development software tools and systems development terminology. A member of the development staff often serves in this role. To design these sessions, sketch out the steps that need to be taken to produce the session product and then use normal Person-Centred Management techniques to derive them.

A Data Modelling Session

Never conduct a data modelling session without an Electronic Meeting System!

To construct a data model, especially at a corporate level, you must pull vast amounts of information from a variety of people in your organisation. The information and the interviewees' perspectives range from the highest level visions to the most minute detail. You absolutely must have the power of an electronic meeting facility to collect, organise, filter, edit, and to keep the participants' attention.

For data modelling, I use the following three questions to gather information:

1. Who do you do business with?

2. What information or physical objects pass between each of these people and you?

3. What pieces of information are contained on or about these things that pass between you?

The Person-Centred Manager works through a few examples with the entire group and then each participant works at his or her own pace. As they complete various steps, the data modeler gathers the input and edits it. She posts any questions she has and then the Person-Centred Manager guides the group through a review with the modeler. All of this is accomplished with electronic meeting software. Besides the direct benefits during the session, you are able to load previous work into the tool to start with and to transfer the session products directly into data modelling software afterwards.

I initially tried it with the data modeler facilitating, but found it better to have the roles played by two people because of the amount of concentration each activity requires. Person-Centred Managers need to be familiar with the data modelling process and products, but do not need to be modelers themselves.

Question Lists

A Person-Centred Manager can seldom have too many questions. I recommend keeping a variety of question lists to use with your group. As you design your session, you may find it advisable to work from these lists, particularly when neither of you has clarity on products or outcomes. You usually find one of your question lists is perfect for use by the group when you are in session. Once you have a variety of lists, it is easy to tailor lists of questions appropriate for your current Person-Centred Management session.

General Question List

1. What opportunities are possible in our situation?

2. How can I adapt to this change?

3. How can I improve the way I do business?

4. What else can I produce with the skills and resources I already have?

5. How can I make this system/procedure/product/service better?

6. What are some other uses for this?

7. If I do this, what could go wrong?

8. How can I resolve this difficult, complex, or unusual problem?

9. How can I gain support for this initiative?

10. How can I turn this negative situation to our advantage?

11. What impact will this idea, programme, or system have on our employees or customers?

Process Improvement Question List

1. Who are our suppliers and customers in this process?

2. Which features of our products and/or services are most important to them?

3. What characteristics of our products or services could be improved?

4. What operations have the greatest effect on our products or services?

5. How does performance of our operations need to change?

6. How will it impact our existing systems?

7. Have I got any complaints from our customers in the last three months?

8. Has anyone talked to our customers in the last three months about our products or services?

9. What's going wrong that I can fix right now?

10. How much will it cost?

Strategic Planning Question List

1. What do I do best?

2. Who are our customers?

3. Who will our customers be in the future?

4. Will our products or services be the same?

5. Does our organisational culture support the critical areas of our business?

6. Where's our organisation headed?

7. Am I controlling our organisation's direction? If not, why not? What might I do about it?

8. What are the key factors in our success so far? Am I supporting these factors? If so, how? If not, why not? What, if anything, must I change in order to have everyone in the organisation focus on them?

Organisation Self Analysis Question List

1. Why am I in business?

2. What are our basic products or services?

3. Who are our primary customers of these products or services?

4. What major activities are involved in providing each product or service?

5. Who provides us with information, material, services to help us do our job or provide our products or services?

6. What are the two things they do well? How does that help us do our job?

7. What's one thing I would change if I could? How would the change help us do our job better?

8. What things do I do that aren't directly related to the products or services we're in business to provide? Why do I do them? Should I continue doing them? What do I need to do to stop doing them?

9. How do I evaluate success? Does it compliment or conflict with what our customers want or need? What could I evaluate that might be more meaningful? How can I shift our focus?

10. What changes could I make that would provide higher customer satisfaction? What would delight them?

11. What's currently helping us or preventing us from providing the best possible products or services to our customers? How can I reduce or eliminate hindrance and build on the helpers?

12. What's currently helping us become a high performing

organisation?

13. What's hindering our becoming a high performing organisation?

14. How can I reduce or eliminate hindrance and build on the helpers to become a high performing organisation?

CHAPTER 10

Electronic Meeting Systems and Accelerated Learning Techniques

In this chapter you will learn:

How your company can best benefit
by using the latest technology
How to create an environment which promotes
creativity and facilitates accelerated learning

Scented markers were great, the Wack Pack added a lot of fun, and Smart Boards made our socks roll up and down, but the most exciting addition to the Person-Centred Manager's tool kit this century has been the development of **Electronic Meeting Systems** (EMS). Electronic Meeting Systems are technology-based environments that support group meetings. The system may include facilities, hardware, software, video and audio, and group work methods.

The good news is that it makes some of the hardest parts of managing sessions easy and has completely redefined the opportunities for groups working together.

How does it work?

Electronic Meeting Systems include software that runs on a computer network. Each participant in a session has a workstation through which they communicate. The input of the participants is combined and can be sent to other participants, the Person-Centred Manager and projection devices.

EMS software contains tools that automate all standard Person-Centred Management session techniques. Some of the current capabilities are:

- Brainstorming

- Comment on topics

- Organising ideas

- Group writing

- Group Voting

- Checking the mood meter

- Uploading and downloading information

104

Information can be uploaded into the EMS software or you can start from scratch. The briefcase stores reference material and pre-session products for easy access during the session. With Windows versions, you can access other software tools, like spreadsheets, calculators and wordprocessors, from within the EMS.

The information gathered in any of the tools can be ported easily into any other tool. For instance, you may produce a list in Brainstormer and then pull it into the editor to clean it up, removing redundancies and clarifying terms. You can then put it into group vote for the group to prioritise. A variety of voting methods are pre-programmed and standard statistical summaries are available. You may then move the newly ordered list into group editor for work, or, split it up and have people comment on selected items in topic commentor.

This ability to transfer information across tools, almost instantly, enables you to lead groups through processes that you may not currently think possible. You and the group no longer need to be victims of information overload!

At the end of the session, you can download or print any of the session products.

Electronic Meeting Systems are most commonly used for same-time/same-place meetings, with all participants in an EMS facility. The meetings are led by a Person-Centred Manager and the software and session recording is managed by a technographer. Complete knowledge of the tool set is required of both. Special Person-Centred Manager training, or extensive experience, is necessary for a Person-Centred Manager to take advantage of Electronic Meeting System capabilities and to manage the group dynamics that appear in that setting.

In addition to same-time/same-place meetings, meetings can be held at distributed locations and can take place over extended periods of time. As an example, a manager might post a number of issues for discussion on EMS software and gather input for days or weeks or even all year! These variations are called same-time/different-place and different-time/different-place meetings.

Changes in Group Dynamics as a result of EMS

Probably the most radical change to the group process is caused by the fact that participants contribute anonymously. A manager must be prepared to hear the truth if choosing to have a session with electronic meeting software. This is a wonderful way to get to the real heart of issues, but both the company and the Person-Centred Manager must be prepared for it.

Remember the introverts? Those people who can have trouble in a group setting because they think before they speak? Their day has come with electronic meetings, especially if they learned to type while the extroverts were talking. The introverts now have the time and quiet to think and they do not have to fight for the talking stick. They just think things through and enter them on their workstation.

I noticed extreme extroverts, those who really need to interact externally to think, had some trouble getting started and sticking with the task and needed special help from the Person-Centred Manager.

The speed at which the group can work is another big change in the electronic environment. To be effective, it is more important than ever for the Person-Centred Manager to know exactly what they're going to do with the output of each step in the process they designed. With Electronic Meeting Systems, a new breed of PCM has been spawned.

The number of people who can participate, even in highly creative steps, has multiplied. The Ten to Twelve Rule flies out the window in managed electronic meetings. EMS Person-Centred Managers report success with forty to fifty participants where the limit used to be a dozen. Again, the Person-Centred Manager must be adept at knowing what to do with all of that information as it begins flowing.

Participants are more active and prolific. If you participate in a manually facilitated session with nine other people and the session lasts four hours, the average amount of air time you will get eighteen minutes. In an electronic meeting you may get an hour or two.

Those who can't type are at a distinct disadvantage. This may intimidate some of your participants, and it may reverse the power chain in the session, so be prepared!

What's Good About It?

- It speeds things up! Immeasurably.

- It manages one of the hardest things about manual Person-Centred Management sessions, that is, trying to organise and refine the information you are gathering without losing the interest of the participants.

- It allows anonymity and the real facts can come out.

- It removes the ability of an individual to dominate a session.

- It eliminates group size restrictions.

- It allows introverts time to think.

Why do I need to know about it?

- Because it is the meeting environment of the future.

- Because electronic meetings still require master Person-Centred Managers.

- Because it will make your job easier.

- Because your bosses are going to start hearing about it and demanding it.

The more connections that can be made in the brain, the more integrated the experience is within memory.

As you gain experience managing sessions, you will begin to expand your awareness of what's possible working with groups.

Your mastery of basic skills will give you the confidence you need to try new inventions. This chapter is about increasing creativity in the managed session by enhancing the environment. It is based on accelerated or enhanced learning principles.

I anticipate your questions so I will use the structured question and answer format to explain these principles to you.

Q: What is accelerated learning?
Accelerated or enhanced learning (AL) is a multi-sensory, holistic approach to learning that describes the conditions for learning and the presentation of material. It uses the whole brain approach to learning, that is, AL techniques engage both the left and right brain. AL develops skills and knowledge through the physical, emotional, social and psychological aspects of being. The learner is viewed as an interactive player. Techniques are used to deliberately stimulate the senses. Materials are presented in creative ways that are compatible with our senses and engages them.

Q: Why would I want to apply accelerated learning to human resources?
Researchers have found that people work and learn more effectively in a positive, emotionally supportive environment. AL techniques take anxiety and competition out of the environment and replaces them with positive energy, positive speaking and collaboration. Using AL techniques means I manage the conditions that enhance learning and reduce barriers that impede learning.

As the name implies, using these techniques accomplishes the task or learning in a much shorter time than by using conventional methods. Person-Centred Management sessions are very intense for short periods of time (one-half to three days), and often require numerous products. Techniques that can accelerate the group's working together in the easiest way and producing the highest quality products are beneficial to everyone.

Q: How do I apply it?
Simple - you bring the environment with you. Once you get

the hang of it, you will probably need a steamer trunk! Remember, this is a multi-sensory approach, you engage all the senses - hearing, seeing, touching, tasting and smelling. AL focuses on engagement of the unconscious mind to accelerate and enhance learning. Everything from the room to the materials to your own attitude becomes part of the AL environment.

Specifically, I recommend you discuss your approach with your colleagues so there will be no surprises when you begin your session. Even if they only agree to limited AL techniques, your Person-Centred Management sessions will be enhanced. Research has demonstrated that people work and learn faster and easier in a relaxed, playful environment. However, not everyone yet understands the enhancement process and its application to the business world. Success breeds success and as you gain expertise, AL can further enhance your service to others.

Here are some of the basic AL concepts with specific how to's for managing sessions.

- Provide a natural, comfortable and colourful setting. Co-ordinate the various colours you use for your materials so the overall effect is pleasing.

- Secure the most comfortable and attractive facilities available.

- Place plants and flowers around the environment.

- Provide a refreshment table with light snacks such as fruits and cheeses and have a variety of beverages available, including water.

- Use coloured pens (scented if possible), papers and folders. Buy clear crystal plastic cups to hold the coloured pens.

- Personally greet participants and learn their names.

Reduce or eliminate fears, anxieties or barriers:

- Do a guided relaxation.

- Use imagery.

- Play background music.

- Project a relaxed, fun, caring attitude.

- Use an oil burner with a pleasing fragrance such as vanilla or essential oils like orange or geranium.

- Use a simple physical game to energise everyone.

Make what you do fun rather than serious and overbearing:

- Use 'props' such as stuffed toys, crazy games, balloons or weird gadgets that can be played with during a break.

- Use poster board instead of flip chart paper. Decorate it.

- Create 'doodle mats' for participants to colour, using pictures and words from the session theme.

Be positive and accepting:

- Eliminate negative words while you speak. Say 'It is easy to' not 'This is hard work'. Say 'I have an ambitious agenda', not 'I have a lot to do today, I hope I can get it all done'.

Exalt rather than criticise participants:

- Bring inexpensive gifts, wrapped in paper decorated with the session theme, and give them out for something special. What's special? Don't worry — you will know. Here is an example. For a Connections theme, I used metal paper clips strung together and taped one end to the bottom of a small jewellry sized box and the other end to the lid. When the box was opened it produced a fun effect. I purchased plastic multicolored paper clips and stick pins for gifts. Everybody loved the gifts as a play on the theme Connections.

Present material pictorially as well as verbally.

- For a team building session, print out quotes or sayings about teamwork and mount them on coloured paper and hang them on the walls or doors.

- Use theme pictures on any view graphs or handouts.

- Use inexpensive posters, plastic mats, colourful calendars, etc. that capture session, products or theme ideas.

Suggested supply and equipment list:

- Transparencies and transparency markers

- Masking tape

- Clear tape

- 3x5 self-sticking notes

- Overhead projector

- TV and VCR

- Plain paper

- Regular ink pens

- Pastel pens and markers, preferably scented

- Big markers for easels, various colours

- Coloured file folders

- Coloured paper

- Plants

- Flowers

- Simmering pot

- Relaxation tapes

- Tape player

- Sayings mounted on coloured 400x500mm heavy paper

- Clear plastic cups to hold pens

- Place mats with words and pictures designed from agenda items

- Sweets

- Crystal ball

- Magic cards (playing cards) made from poster board

- Light bulb visual on poster board for Brainstorming

- Visual theme for agenda, wrapping paper, etc

- Gifts that tie into the theme

- Creative Wack Pack (tools including sticky signs, perfumed oils, cloud-shaped cards, pencils etc.) and basket to hold them in

- Hats - great props for participants and you

- Stuffed toys

- Silly, crazy gadgets to play with over breaks

- Camera and film

CHAPTER 11

Anatomy of a Session

In this chapter we see

What constitutes a good meeting

Why meetings are perceived as unsuccessful

How to plan a meeting or creativity session

The goal and responsibility of a Person-Centred Manager is to provide the atmosphere, tools and techniques that allows a *good* working Person-Centred Management sessions to occur. Now let us take a look at one core activity at the heart of all working environments - meetings

Knowing some basic facts about meetings, and how people feel about attending them, allows you to 'design in' success.

In my interviews, people have expressed what they find distasteful about meetings:

- I didn't know why I was there.

- Mr/Ms X started in again and talked and talked until the meeting finally ended.

- It dragged on and on.

- I had more important things to do.

- Like most of our meetings, it just led to another meeting.

- I kept getting interrupted.

- No decision was made.

- Information from the meeting wasn't passed on to the people who needed it.

- As usual, everyone left with a different opinion of what happened.

- The decision was made before the meeting, so I do not know why I had to meet at all.

- No one followed up on anything.

- As usual, a couple of people got all of the work and they weren't the right people.

- I didn't really accomplish anything because I didn't have

what I needed to do the work.

- I never get the meeting started on time.

- I have a lot of meetings and I never have everyone there, so none of our decisions last.

- The real problems are avoided.

People have expressed the following traits of *good* meetings:

- Short

- To the point

- It was clear what the meeting was about.

- I made a decision.

- I stuck to the agenda.

- People listened to what I had to say.

- My boss listened to what I had to say.

- I finished what I set out to do.

- I decided what needed to be done quickly, then everyone took part of the task and I did the work outside of the meeting. I didn't meet again until all of that was done.

- I found out what each other was doing.

- I felt involved.

The good news is that there are techniques for improving all of the conditions that can lead to a distasteful or non-productive meeting. That's what Person-Centred Management is all about! The rest of this book is a tool kit loaded with techniques I've found to work.

The key to successful person centred meetings or sessions is planning and preparation. I call this *session design*.

Your design will provide a framework or a structure that will optimise the participants' time together, allows a way for people to talk to each other constructively, and produces the desired products of the meeting. Before the session actually occurs, its success or failure may have already been determined by its design.

Person-Centred session design includes meeting with your company boss to determine its essence or purpose, designing the work process for the group, and designing the environment in which the group will work.

How you approach design will vary with your own personal style and experience as well as the complexity of the session you are leading. An advanced Person-Centred Manager may feel comfortable going through the entire design process with the company boss during the initial interview. Those less experienced may need to do the work process design after the interview and then finalise it in a follow-on meeting.

Meeting with your team

This initial meeting with your team, colleagues or peers is very important for all of you. It gives each of you the opportunity to get acquainted as well as to explore the reasons for the session. Be aware that you will be evaluated then which will determine how much they trust you. The more relaxed and confident you are, the deeper the level of trust that can develop between you.

Anyone doing a Person-Centred session must be very clear about their own beliefs. Our assumptions about organisations determine, in subtle ways, our own facilitating style and the skills with which I work. For example, if you think staff problems may be solved by participating in more and collaborative groups, then you must be collaborative and participate more with your client to earn his or her trust.

To begin with, there are two questions that are the most important you need to ask. Always! They are the questions you ask first, before you discuss anything else.

116

1. What do you want as session outcomes?

2. What do you want as session products?

Outcomes will usually be general in nature. You might like to think of outcomes as things that can't be measured. An example would be your company needing employees to operate like a team instead of the current **I-they** style in use. Your company might describe the desired outcome as "I want everyone working together like one big happy family."

The products your company needs are more tangible and measurable than outcomes. Examples are a vision statement or plan of action, or, less tangibly, a discussion on role clarification or expectations each member has of the group.

Until you get clear answers to these questions, designing the session is impossible.

After you and your colleagues come to an understanding of what each of you need and expect from the other, work process design begins.

Work Process Design

Designing the work process for a Person-Centred session is a learned art. You need a solid knowledge of group dynamics and available tools and techniques in order to do it. Experience also plays an important role in becoming a good designer. Here are the basic steps to follow in the session design process.

1. Clarify the purpose of the meeting.

2. Define the desired outcomes and products.

3. Determine who should attend.

4. Design the sequence of meeting activities.

a. Pick a method for each step.

b. Review and adjust your design by asking:

Can I get from one step to the next smoothly?

Are all steps necessary?

How much time will it take?

Will these methods work for this group?

Is there anything about this method or topic that could blow up?

5. Decide how to begin and how to conclude the session.

6. Determine logistics, equipment and administrative needs.

7. Complete the agenda.

8. Finalise the design with your client.

During *work process design*, keep these factors in mind:

Group size
The number of participants will affect your methods. Groups larger than five automatically take on the traits of hierarchy. To produce highly creative products, you may want to break the participants into subgroups of five or less.

Groups of ten to twelve may not need to be broken into smaller groups for simple sessions, such as idea generation or dialogue.

Electronic meeting software (see Chapter 10) changes the rules on group size, allowing much larger groups to take on activities than are not possible in a manual Person-Centred Management session.

Gathering lots of information
When you are hosting multiple sessions that produce large amounts of information, schedule a day or two in between sessions so that you can manage the products of each one and prepare properly for the next.

Draft products

When it's appropriate, use a draft product for the group to work with. Make a list of action items which have to be attended to, listing who is to do them and by when. Use Data Modelling tools which are IT programmes designed to produce physical material from sessions. Use printed materials with innovative ideas listed out, or brochures to get the session going. Starting from scratch can be a slow, tedious process for a group and most sessions benefit from a more robust beginning. Using draft products honours any work that was accomplished before the session and develops a positive environment. Later use tools to list outcomes so that participants get a sense of satisfaction from something achieved. They may be apparently intangible benefits like contentment, better communications occurring, shared knowledge, a speeding of information, but they are worth listing to feel a sense of achievement and highlight what needs to be nurtured in future. Exceptions to this are sessions where a fresh start is exactly what is called for. Visioning, for example, is a process that would not benefit from the influence of a draft product.

Sequencing activities

Block out time to produce each product. Remember that most people need to speak to stay involved. Allow for that in your calculations. Timing will always be a 'guesstimate.' Don't be surprised if something you thought would take less time actually takes longer and vice versa. There is a variety of techniques discussed in Chapter 10 that will assist you in managing time.

Restating purpose

Even with detailed communication about the purpose of the session between the participants and yourself, do not be surprised to have participants arriving at your session wondering: Why am I here?, What's going to happen?, What's expected of me? Participants will seldom ask these questions. No one wants to appear uninformed. Trust us, it's happening and the group can't perform until fears rising from these unanswered questions are eased. At the beginning of the Person-Centred session, build in a few minutes to formally explain the purpose of the session. Solicit questions after the explanation.

Mid-course correction

You may find the need to change your methods or the schedule during the session. That's okay. It's still important to have an initial plan to get the group centred and comfortable with the process. Even though you may have to change the agenda or methodology, the planned framework allows you to always know what has to be done. You know the bottom line requirements — Outcomes, products and available time.

Use positive words

Frequently, colleagues request a number of products for one session. I recommend you describe a session that's going to produce a variety of products as one having a *challenging agenda*. Comments to the group like 'I have a lot of work to do today' or 'This is going to be a tough day' are discouraging and set the session up as one of drudgery. Negative comments like this will drain participants' energy before they begin.

Breakout group assignments

If you decide to divide the group into subgroups, you may want to make subgroup assignments before the session to save time. The list can be handed out with the agenda. If there are participants who have chronic personal conflicts, this allows them to be separated. For product delivery, it may be necessary to spread a mixture of knowledge, skills and abilities throughout each of the breakout groups.

Post-session completion

Post-session work is not the job of the Person-Centred Manager. Advise your colleagues about the session design to include the following:

1. For your session to have lasting impact, each participant may need to receive the documented output of the session as soon as possible.

2. Ensure any follow-up actions, including the completed session documentation, have been assigned before the session ends. Suggest that a co-ordinator be appointed

and who it should be.

3. If outputs include a task list or actions, make sure a group member's name and phone number is placed on this work. This allows the member to be contacted if clarification is needed.

Designing the Environment

The planning stage of a Person-Centred session must also consider the requirements for space, equipment and support.

The Meeting Room

Secure a meeting room and look at:

Atmosphere: Is the room cheerful in colour and does it have outside windows?

Layout: Is the room large enough for your needs? Will everyone be able to see the items you work with and each other?

Furniture: Are the chairs comfortable for longer meetings?

Conveniences: How far away are the rest rooms, smoking areas, lunchroom, elevators and food?

Lighting: Is there sufficient lighting? Can the room be darkened easily?

Noise: Is the room free of excessive noise and interruptions? Will everyone be able to hear what's going on?

Outlets: Are there enough electrical points for equipment?

Heat & Cooling: Will the temperature be appropriate and can you control it yourself?

Telephone: Is there a phone nearby for participants to use privately? Is there one in the room? Do you want it there? The answer is generally NO.

One of the most important things during a session is for

everyone to be able to see and hear everything that's going on. Otherwise you will lose them and their good ideas.

The room should support good projection for your tools. If you use a computer display, make sure that the contents are large enough and coloured correctly for everyone to see easily. You also need the screen area dark enough so that people can read the screen, and the rest of the room light enough so that 1) the materials you are working with can be seen, 2) people can see each other, and 3) people do not fall asleep.

Most organisations have modern meeting rooms designed with good lighting systems. Plan the session early enough to reserve the best facilities. If possible, visit the room before the session and make necessary adjustments to lighting and the size and colours of your display products.

If you plan to use flip chart paper, ensure that there is plenty of wall space to display all products during the session.

Equipment, Supplies and Support

The following lists identify the most commonly needed items:

Equipment Checklist

- Flip chart easels

- Extension cords and pole strips

- Overhead projector

- Screen

- Tape recorder for music

- VCR

- Television set
- Whiteboard

- Computers

- Printers

- Extra tables for overhead projector, materials, group breakout areas

Supply Checklist

- Transparencies

- Blank paper

- Extra flip chart paper

- Folders

- Big marker pens (lots of colours)

- Coloured, scented pens

- Masking and transparent tape

- Pencils and pens

- Scissors

- Stapler

- Transparency pens, Whiteboard markers and erasers

- Large self-sticking notes for all the participants

Support Checklist

- A person to record the session.

- A refreshment table in the room providing light snacks and drinks.

- Transportation for participants if necessary.

- Travel arrangements

CHAPTER 12

Preparing and Delivering a Session

This chapter will outline

The necessary steps to ensure a successful meeting or session

How to arrange a room for maximum benefit

How to run a meeting or session so that all participants can maximise their contribution

Now that you have planned your session and designed the agenda, methods and schedule that you think will work best, it is time to arrange for the facilities, tools, and support you need. Like good planning, preparation is critical to the success of the session.

Remember that by deciding to host a person-centred session, your company is showing willingness to invest in a productive and special way of working. Do not demean them or yourself by skimping on resources. You are the expert and the company expects you to let them know what is necessary to accomplish your work.

Preparing the Participants

For your session to go well, people need to know beforehand what the session is about and what's expected of them. They also may need background information and materials. It is not the Person-Centred Manager's responsibility to produce all of these, but it is your responsibility to advise your company that it needs to be done.

The Person-Centred Manager will supply the session agenda and advise the company to prepare an invitation letter and any background information or draft products. These are either given to participants before the session or at the session, depending on which is more appropriate to the company's needs.

In interviews with managers who have used PM sessions, I have learned that a common mistake is not properly preparing the participants. Many people find working in a group atmosphere uncomfortable, and it is the Person-Centred Manager's responsibility to prepare them psychologically for the event. This may mean having a preparatory meeting or discussion, viewing an inspiring video tape together, or involving them in preparation work.

It is often advisable to have draft work for the group to work with in the session. Groups have even more difficulty than individuals starting from a blank sheet of paper. Encourage your colleagues to work on draft products with you, if appropriate, and make sure you are familiar with the contents. This also honours work that has occurred before. It can alleviate resentment from anyone who has worked on this problem before who now feels their work has been rejected or that no progress has been made and "We're just re-inventing the wheel!"

How to Arrange a Room

There are several choices for setting up the room for optimal communications. Room arrangements set expectations and can create a more comfortable, relaxed feeling among the participants. Clustered seating encourages collaborative interactions with group members.

The most commonly used arrangement is a U-shaped table for participants with the Person-Centred Manager working at the open end of the U. This arrangement is important for democratic, drop-the-rank interaction. Everybody can see the faces of the other participants and there are no built-in power positions at the table.

While the U is optimal for most meetings, sometimes there are too many people for the U and you may have to deviate somewhat. If you need a U-shaped configuration, hold out for a room that can support it.

U-Shape: Form tables in a U-shape with chairs on the outside. The open part of the U is for presentation.

Semicircle: Place a flip chart on an easel in the open end of the semicircle.

Round Table: If there will be a lot of writing, use a large round table. Leave a space open at the table for presentation materials. This also works well if the Person-Centred Manager will be seated.

Herringbone: This is a variation you can use when you need a U-shape and there isn't room. Arrange two sets of tables in a herringbone shape with chairs on the outside only. The Person-Centred Manager and equipment can face these two tables.

Elevated, Stair-stepped, U-Shape: Electronic meeting facilities for large groups are often arranged in this auditorium style with the workstations arranged along raised, curved rows. The Person-Centred Manager is in the front at the lowest level with sophisticated projection systems. The deviation of the U-shape is successful because the electronic meeting process and software tools enlivens the attention and participation of the group.

Rows: If you walk into a room to manage a session and see this arrangement, change it immediately. If you are told you cannot change it, what are your options?

1. Run screaming from the room.

2. Refuse to manage.

3. Re-read option number two.

4. Get very inventive fast.

People need to look at each other to work together. Recent studies have shown that 55% of our communication is through body language and 38% is through tone of voice. Only 7% is verbal or what I actually say. If people are aligned in rows, they'll miss over half of what's being communicated!

Person-Centred Management Tools

As a Person-Centred Manager, your speciality is guiding a group of people to a succinct, accepted, supported product from a myriad of facts and opinions. You need the right tools to do this.

Person-Centred Managers can fall into the trap of becoming so comfortable with one tool or technique that they use it in all circumstances whether it is appropriate or not. It's like learning to use a screwdriver and then viewing every problem as a set of loose screws. In fact, the solution may require pliers or a wrench or a jackhammer.

As a Person-Centred Manager, it is important to become familiar with all available tools, from the most time-honoured and simple to the newest that technology offers. You then select the appropriate tools for the conditions.

New Technologies

Information technology is producing new tool sets every day and I advise you to become familiar and comfortable with them. You can read about them in trade magazines, but computer trade shows or visits to places that use them, are the best place to see them and try them out. Conferences in your technical speciality often have vendor shows in conjunction with them.

New tools on the market

Smart boards: The contents of a white board are either printed directly from the board or are inserted into word-processing or graphics software.

Pen-based technology: The pen you use on a projection screen or board is software-smart and sends commands like "close this document", "expand into detail" or "move this item to the display".

Modelling software: Software tools that graphically depict modelling work produced in session.

Electronic meeting systems: Software and projection systems that automate and improve the basic set of managed functions such as brainstorming, editing, categorising, generating lists and ideas, providing background documents and voting.

Like all Person-Centred Management methods, benefits depend on what it is you are trying to accomplish and who your participants are.

If you are considering the use of automated tools in your session, please consider the following trade offs:

Benefits:
• Can speed up the session and keep things neat.

- Participants leave with their own copy of session products.

- Allows bigger than flip chart paper products like matrices or models.

- Can reduce or eliminate post-session work.

- Can get to the final product quicker, often before the end of the session.

Considerations:

- May distract participants if used inappropriately.

- May intimidate participants, depending on their background.

- Changes the tone and focus of the group.

- Requires a software expert and equipment.

Simple Use of a Wordprocessor and Projection

I have used simple automation very effectively by keeping it unobtrusive. A person, called a scribe, who is adept at taking notes, puts everything that is happening on the board into a word processor. This is done in the background to avoid distraction. As you produce lists on flip charts or an overhead, they are recorded page-by-page by the scribe. These pages can then be printed and passed out to participants as needed.

Reworking of flip chart items can be very messy. Doing this rework on a word processor or transparency projected overhead is much easier. If you use this approach, make sure your scribe is very fast with the software and comfortable with what is expected of him. He or she needs to be familiar with the terminology and acronyms that the group will be using. It is beneficial to have a practice session with the scribe before the session to work out potential problems such as what could happen, how the information should be captured and displayed, how the two of you will communicate in the session, how big the text should be and how to print.

Use projection of a computer screen selectively for work such as brainstorming, sorting or refining work that has been done. When on-line work becomes visible, with software that isn't designed specifically for group work, the entire group dynamic can change. you will learn through experience when the use of technology is effective and when it is a distraction.

Conducting a session

Congratulations! The big day has arrived. All of your planning and preparation has allowed you to walk into the session with confidence. You know you have everything you need to help this group realise its purpose. You may think that statement is very idealistic and that it doesn't allow for surprises or for human error. It does! Faith in your abilities and intent, and trust in yourself, others and the environment, will supply you with whatever you need. It is guaranteed.

Beginning the Session

Most people feel nervous about speaking in front of groups. In the United States this is people's number one fear. Fear of death is number seven, which means that most people are more afraid to speak in public than they are to die! I point this out to help you acknowledge the humaness of your apprehension and that other participants will experience the same discomfort, as they, too, know they will be asked to speak.

I recommend that before the session begins, you walk around and meet and greet everyone and briefly visit with them in a light-hearted way. This simple act immediately begins relieving any fears, both yours and theirs. It allows all of you to begin to get acquainted, share your humaness and create an initial level of trust. If someone offers to help you do something, like test the overhead projector, let them. Most people enjoy helping others and it does not mean they think you are incapable of the task.

All sessions need an introductory segment. The form this takes will depend on the session design and your style. The introductory segment will always include the actions listed below:

- Introductory Remarks/Ice-Breaker

- Acknowledge and thank the group for their participation.

- Explain your role as Person-Centred Manager.

- State the purpose of the session.

- If an agenda is used, explain it.

- State desired outcomes and products for the session.

- Develop group norms.

Your style and the company's preferences will determine the form of your introduction.

I would like to discuss four key parts of the session's agenda in detail - **the agenda, ice-breakers, group norms** and **the role of the Person-Centred Manager.** These items are critical to the success of the session. Doing the ice-breaker and group norms segments may feel awkward for both you and the participants because they are not something you do every day.

The Session Agenda
It is always advisable to give the group a prepared agenda. It becomes the road map for your working together. Everyone has their own style of thinking - a visual, auditory or feeling orientation. All of us can do each of these, I just prefer one over the other. Providing a visual agenda, as well as talking through the agenda, ensures more people are clear about the session structure. People who prefer the feeling style will just know!

I have learned it is best to keep the agenda very simple. do not structure it with attached times for each portion of work or breaks. People who find comfort in clear-cut delineations of time become very uncomfortable if the advertised time schedule isn't met. By avoiding exact times for each portion of the session, there are no time expectations and no time pressures!

Ice-breakers

Sometimes when you begin a session, no formal ice-breaker is needed. Even so, it will be to your advantage to begin with humour or something light-hearted to help remove any tensions (both yours and session participants). Getting yourself and your group 'off on the right foot' is an essential part of group dynamics. Just going around and giving one's name and title isn't sufficient. In fact, I recommend leaving titles out of the introductions to set the stage for more democratic participation.

Structured warm-up activities, even if very casual, help participants get involved more quickly, increase their energy and interest, and get acquainted with each other if they haven't met.

Often, your boss will provide humour or a humourous event to begin the session. Most people have a great sense of humour and want to come across as 'real', especially bosses who generally maintain a more formal image in their organisational role as leader.

Ideas for Ice-Breakers

Here are some ideas for ice-breakers I have used successfully and can recommend:

1. Write a note to all participants before the session. This works well if you are going off-site for several days. If the session has a theme, it is easy to take the theme and work something about it into your note to them. Be sure to tell them about yourself and your qualifications, but do it in a light-hearted way.

2. A funny set of test questions may be appropriate, especially if you are going to be doing things that are new to them, like **team building** or process improvement. The questions can be teaching points. Few people may know the actual answers, so you can make the multiple choice answers silly to make

everyone laugh and feel comfortable.

3. If the people do not know each other, use the beginning of the session to have them get acquainted.

One way is to have them pair up and introduce each other. After a two to three minute interview for each partner, they each introduce the other. This alleviates the tension surrounding introductions as it is much easier to introduce another person than it is yourself.

4. Go around the table and ask each person to state their expectations for this meeting.

5. Before the session begins, introduce yourself to as many people as you can. If an ice-breaker isn't appropriate, this is probably the best way to 'break the ice' for both you and the participants.

6. You may be able to set up something either with your colleagues or someone you might know who is part of the group. One of the easiest to do is a question plant. Using whatever humour is appropriate or an event that has just happened to them, talk briefly, and then ask if anyone has a question. Your plant will ask it and you can create laughter. Also, current news events are often appropriate.

7. Often, the environment in which you find yourself has exactly what you need to release tension. I can't tell you what that is, these are instant creations you will discover yourself! Our advice is to be open and use whatever presents itself. If you believe the statement, "All my needs are always met", they will be. I do and it always works.

To summarise, the reasons for having an ice-breaker can include:

• Helping to clarify group members' expectations and knowledge.

• Introducing participants to working within a group.

• Enhancing interpersonal relationships.

• Relieving anxiety.

You may want to start a file of ideas as you discover them so that you have a variety to choose from for different types of sessions. There are books available which will give you ideas for ice-breakers. Other Person-Centred Managers or trainers are also a good source of ideas. Always adapt these activities to fit the session and group members' needs.

Group Norms

In the introductory portion of the session, you will lead the group in developing the norms for their behaviour. Either your colleague will name them to support a theme or the group will name them in the session. I often call them **House Rules.**

House Rules are developed by the participants and written out and prominently displayed during the session. Not only are they norms for the participants, they're your norms as well.

You begin by asking the group to develop the rules under which they, as a group, desire to guide their behaviour during the session. You might wish to ask them to think about the following two questions as they decide what would be effective rules for the group:

1. What behaviours do you feel are important to achieve success for this meeting?

2. What behaviours would you like others to exhibit and to which you are also willing to commit?

Person-Centred Managers and group members may feel uncomfortable the first time they develop norms. Do not be surprised if you feel this way also. Know that groups appreciate having these rules and will develop them. Often simply generating this list is all that is needed to create a framework of order for the session. There are several reasons for this. If the group works together daily, the list allows everyone to agree on rules for this particular meeting. If there have been interpersonal conflicts, this list can suspend fears about conflicts arising during this session. If the group doesn't know each other, it allows them to create a framework that can avoid any potentially troublesome personal behaviours. One important rule to remember when you are creating House

Rules is to record the participants' ideas exactly as stated to you. If you are unclear about the wording or it doesn't flow easily, ask the person to repeat the idea. Often, this is all that's needed for the person to restate the idea or the group will help the person develop a clearer statement if they also like it.

I suggest you prepare the format in advance. You may receive a couple of desired norms from your boss like "I want them to have fun or I want honesty". You can have these printed up and allow the group members to develop the rest. The following is an example used in a session:

House Rules
- Exercise trust, openness, and honesty

- Focus on solution and resolution

- Be open to new ways of thinking

- One conversation at a time

- Everyone stays on time

- Have fun

If you have developed a theme for the session, it is easy to use the theme as part of group norms. Here is an example: the theme is about going out into the future. Space ships are being used for the visual representation. The House Rules become 'Crew Rules.' The visual emblem designed for the theme goes with the words "Crew Rules.' If a rocket ship blasting off is the visual, draw the ship and write 'Crew Rules' on the flip chart paper. If you use automation, print it out and tape or glue it to the flip chart paper and write the norms on that page.

I highly recommend you begin the development of group norms by stating your own operating position, which is one of confidentiality and non-attribution. Allow discussion on this, if the group desires it, and frequently they do. There are several reasons for this. One is you. If you are unknown, the group may be fearful you will leave and tell others about their behaviours and actions. If they do not trust you, they will hesitate to be open and candid.

The second reason is past management practices. Many people are fearful about speaking what they perceive as their truth because, in the past, they may have been punished in some way by their organisation for their candid behaviour. Our organisations are changing and managers now realise it is important to be open to truthful, empowered employees and involve them in designing an organisation that will survive and thrive.

If you discussed this issue with your boss or colleague in your initial meeting, and he or she indicated a desire to hear the truth, you can ask him or her to talk about this with the group during the development of group norms. Group discussion of this issue with you, the boss, and each other can allow a deep level of trust to begin.

I highly recommend that when you and the group finish developing the group norms, you ask the group to shake hands with the people on either side of them. You shake hands with the persons sitting to the left and right of you to close the circle. This symbolic physical act strengthens the agreement the group just made on paper.

Role of the Person-Centred Manager

Always explain, at the beginning of the session, who you are and what your role is. You understand your role very well by this time, but the group probably does not. Even those participants who have experienced managed sessions need this explanation since management styles and responsibilities differ from session to session.

Tell the group:

- The group is the customer, I am working for you.

- The group is there to talk to each other, not you.

- The group has the answer and the skills to produce it.

- You are there to help manage group overhead.

- You are objective.

- Your responsibility is to protect the process and keep the session on track.

- Your job ends at the end of the session.

- You might have to call 'time outs' if the group is wandering.

- The Hanger and the Task List and what they are for (see Chapter 13).

- You have a tool kit of techniques to help them work their issues.

- How your role relates to their boss or your colleague during the session.

Producing Session Products

Once the initial introductory portion of the agenda has been accomplished, you begin producing the session products. The group will be guided through this by the methods and schedule you developed.

As you do this, you will make any adjustments to the methods and schedule as needed. Your goal is always to deliver the outcomes and products the company requested. Do not hesitate to work with the group on their needs. As you gain experience, you will sense when a break or a change-of-pace activity is needed. If you are not clear, ask the group. Sometimes situations arise that are not anticipated but are one of those golden opportunities for the group to realise success.

Some Person-Centred Managers will advise you to never allow the group to change the agenda. I would like to modify this to "Never change your agenda unless there's a good reason".

Participants sometimes will try to modify the agenda because they are uncomfortable or they do not understand what is happening and where you are heading. Re-clarify the task and the steps you have designed if this happens. Occasionally, a group member may have a need to derail the session, or the Person-Centred Manager, and may use an agenda change as one of its strategies.

If an agenda change is requested, first examine these possibilities and then use your own knowledge of tools and techniques and your feel for how the group is doing before making the change. If your boss is present, he or she decides.

Closing the Session

Close the session by summarising what has occurred. Do it verbally and visually so that everyone sees and hears what has been realised as outcomes and products.

Help put the results of the group's work into an overall, big-picture framework. During the session, the group was doing the parts. You, as Person-Centred Manager, tie the parts together into the whole when you summarise the session. This gives group members a sense of completion and feedback for work well done.

Thank the participants for their efforts and their co-operation with you and each other to make this session so successful, easy and fun. I will not deny that you may experience a difficult session. However, with careful planning and preparation, you seldom will. If you do, process your emotions and let them go. Become objective and this experience will provide you with very valuable lessons.

If your boss is present, turn the session over to him or her for closing remarks.

CHAPTER 13

Tips and Techniques for the Person-Centred Manager

In this chapter we learn

How to deal with problems in meetings and sessions

- How to avoid pitfalls and how to recover from them

- How to reach consensus - eventually

- How the Person-Centred Manager runs the ideal meeting or session using tried and tested techniques as well as flexibility

You have planned, you have prepared, you have followed every bit of advice I've offered. Your equipment is working perfectly, the room couldn't be nicer, the fruit tray looks enticing and your agenda reflects your belief in an ordered universe.

The session begins and you become a self-adjusting, self-correcting process control mechanism. You load your sample-feedback-adjustment programme into your head and keep it running until normal system shutdown!

When you find the following, fast action is required:

Motivation lacking? Motivate them.

Conflict arising? Go Around or intervention.

Low energy? Take a break - do an energising activity.

Hopelessly lost? Get knowledge, quick!

Find the problem-solver.

Summarise and re-clarify the task.

Avoiding the task force and direction.
Create ownership.

Distracting topics, The Hangar (see page 160)

Use a more structured technique.

Low participation, Throw index cards around
Go Around.
Turn the marker over and sit down.

Underlying conflict, Root it out.

Subtle sabotage, Confront.

Got it? What a menagerie of talents a Person-Centred Manager must have! It sounds so complex in a book. Do not worry, it comes together in the session.

I have managed many different kinds of sessions. Every time I do a session, I usually learn one more new thing. I recommend you keep your own file of lessons learned and review them before every meeting. Facilitating is evolutionary. As organisations change, our styles and methods must also change. The purpose of this chapter is to share with you what I have learned, sometimes through trial and error.

> **Rule #1: A Person-Centred Manager ALWAYS remains neutral, objective and fair.**

> **Rule #2: Reread Rule #1!** If you remember nothing else, remember these two rules. They are so important. The moment you stop being neutral and take sides, stop being objective and interject your own opinions, and stop being fair by siding with one person or group over another, you no longer are the Person-Centred Manager. You are just another person running a meeting.

> **Keep everything visible.** It is imperative for keeping people involved.

> **Keep everything recorded.** Do not let ideas evaporate into the air. That is what happens in regular meetings and creates 'a lot of talk with no results.' You need to post every comment, idea or criticism where everyone can see it so it has to be addressed.

You do not have to record every word, just record the idea or fact. You do not have to record it on the product you are currently working on. I begin every session with two lists already hanging in the room. One is **The Hangar** where ideas that are off the point are recorded. The other is **The Task List** where things that need to be done are recorded. Hang them both in the back of the room and when someone brings up an item that belongs on one of them, toss a magic marker to them (not at them!) and have them post it.

Doing this causes a few things to happen. For starters, in order to record the idea, the provider will have to get concise and specific in what they are saying. If you do not understand it well enough to record it, then you need clarification and focus and so does everybody else in the room. The participants will learn quickly that they have to summarise ideas and this behaviour adds clarity, understanding and speed to the entire session.

Once the group sees that everything is getting recorded and will have to be dealt with, they tend to reduce their 'talking for talk's sake' and that helps keep the session moving.

Use colours to clarify changes
When you are making later changes to a list or product, use different colours so that people can see what has changed, or what's new.

Face the group
Learn to use your flip chart or white board or computer so that you are always facing the group.

Involve the participants whenever you can
Meetings are boring when all you do is sit. Many techniques lend themselves to active participation from the group. When designing the work process steps for the session, always question activities that involve the traditional 'I'll stand up front and write, you take turns talking'. These activities can often be done in a style where the participants take a physically active role.

For example, in brainstorming, have participants write their own ideas on large sticky notes, pass them to you and you post them. Besides engaging the group, it speeds up the process.

One of the most powerful aspects of electronic meeting systems is that participants are actively involved throughout the meeting. They talk through their computer and do not have to wait for others to finish.

Do not be afraid to cut off people who are going on and on. This can be hard to do the first couple of times, but you will have to turn in your Person-Centred Manager license if you do not learn it by your second session.

One technique is to suggest The Five Minute Rule during the development of group norms. This is the right for anyone in the session to call 'five minutes' on anyone else if they think the discussion is going on and on and not leading anywhere. State the group's right to call it on you too! Usually it will be used at least once in a session and it is always done with humour. For some reason, this technique 'saves face' of the talker or talkers. Once it is called, its effect seems to last for quite some time.

Honour break times, lunch times, and quitting time.
Your credibility and the trust level the group has for you is put at great risk if you do not honour these times. The only deviation should be at the suggestion and agreement of the group.

Call people by name.
This practice will build trust and a personal relationship between you and your participants. It also makes people feel good, and people who feel good produce better work. Name tags are fine, but if the session lasts more than a day, learn everyone's names without tags. Not being good with names is not an acceptable character flaw for a Person-Centred Manager and will keep you out of the ranks of the experts. If you are not good with names, learn and practise until you are.

Use the space you are in.
Standing allows you to own the space and move easily. However, with the changing work environment, there are times when it is desirable to be seated. Standing can be a power and control tactic and there are situations where that's undesirable. As you become a strong Person-Centred Manager, you will discover you can be even more effective under certain conditions by being seated. Sitting at the end of a table conveys authority. Sitting along the side of the table with participants reduces authority.

Do not favour one side of the room or one section of participants. Often your attention will be drawn to one area of the room or one section of participants. Be on the lookout for that and be sure to look towards, talk to and listen to all portions of the room and audience.

Walk into problem participants. If someone is being destructively aggressive you can temper them by taking advantage of their personal space.

Step away from shy, retiring participants while they speak, but keep your attention focused solely on them so that others will give them time to speak.

The group needs to speak to each other, not to you.
I recommend you always tell people this up front, during your Person-Centred Manager's role introduction. Say something like, "You'll tend to address your comments to me, because I'm standing up front, but it is really each other you want to talk to. You also might seek my approval on ideas since I have the biggest magic marker, but remember, I don't own the outcome, I just care that there is one."

You then need to reinforce this with your actions because the natural tendency is to talk to the person up front. Here are effective ways of redirecting the conversation back to the group:

- If you are asked a question, especially if it is a 'content approval' question, put it out to the group or an individual for answering. Ask "Would anyone like to answer that?" or "I don't know, ask the group". Begin this early in the session and soon participants will skip the middle man (you) and begin addressing each other directly.

- Move behind the speaker. The speaker usually will address the group in front of them instead of turning 180 degrees around to talk to you.

- Look at another group member while you are being spoken to.

- Sit down at the side of the table and direct your focus at the group, away from the speaker.

- A round table or U-shaped configuration naturally encourages conversation within the group.

Know when to be quiet.

The greatest compliment to a Person-Centred Manager is to have the group outgrow them. Remember, high performance groups do not need Person-Centred Managers. Your job won't be at risk until the world has only high performance groups!

There are two factors for you to consider. One is to not build a dependency on you in the first place. The other is to provide the group with tools and experience they can use on their own.

Many Person-Centred Managers build in dependencies on themselves, from the group, through their behaviour. This may happen because the Person-Centred Manager doesn't believe in the inherent intelligence and capability of the group. Telltale behaviours include:

- Allowing the group to address them instead of each other.

- Answering too many **content** questions.

- Not making the work visible and available for everyone.

- Always having to have the answer.

- Unwillingness to release control when the group is doing fine on its own.

- Disrupting progress by taking the group on a tangent or forcing it to do it your way.

- Being closed to suggestions.

To build the group's capability to manage itself, allow its participants every opportunity to accomplish things without you, as soon as they appear to be working together. Start this early in the session if possible.

Do not allow the group to transfer ownership of the process, problem, or recommendation to you.
Some groups do not want to own their problem. That may be the reason the problem couldn't be solved in the normal work environment. Ways to make sure this does not happen are:

- Always be on the lookout for signs that you are being held responsible for the solution.

- When an after-the-session task is identified, have the group assign a responsible person to it.

- When an in-session task arises, like sorting a list, categorising ideas, or editing work, have the group or a sub-group or a participant perform it.

- Do not accept or volunteer for follow-on work from the session.

- Make sure the group addresses all issues raised in the session.

- Follow the guidelines for getting the group to talk to each other.

Read the group and respond.
The group and the individuals in it are giving off continuous signals about their attention level, frustration level, participation level and enjoyment level. Learn to read the energy signals of both the group as a whole and the individual members and take appropriate action. Ask yourself: what am I seeing or what am I sensing? If you are not at present comfortable trusting your intuition, you can learn to trust it. You will sense energy flows of the group or individuals being blocked. Ask yourself why. Trust the first answer that pops into your mind. There may be a need for a break or for a few minutes of talk to clarify a task.

Test your equipment.
Always make sure all of your equipment is working before the session. Nothing turns the group off faster than watching you fight with your equipment.

Reconfirm all arrangements.
Strange understandings can occur at the most unexpected times. Always confirm and reconfirm your facility, equipment and support arrangements. Visit the room after it has been equipped, before the session. Arrive an hour early the first day.

What to do when you don't know what to do.
Ask the group. Enlist them as your allies. you are much more credible if you know when to ask for help. If they invent a technique, it becomes their technique and they love it. Remember, people support what they help create.

Check the mood meter.
Sometimes Person-Centred Managers become so enamoured of the session and its progress and their own excitement and ego that they fail to recognise frustration in the group or in individuals. Learning to read body language and faces is certainly important, but sometimes, just for the heck of it, when everything appears to be peachy, ask something like:

How am I doing?

Am I accomplishing what I want to?

Is the pace right?

Am I getting anywhere?

Do you like the technique we are using?

Are you having fun?

You may be shocked on occasion to find out that things are not as lovely as they appeared. When this happens, the individuals who speak up usually have a constructive solution for fixing the problem, and if you follow it, the group will appreciate your awareness and responsiveness to them.

Never say I told you so.
This is one of the many facets of always preserving the integrity of every individual in every group.

Many times, as a problem solver, you will see, in advance, what the group needs to do to get from here to there. You suggest it and the group will tell you why it won't work. So you do not do it. Then, after a few gyrations of getting nowhere, someone will suggest what you did, the group uses it, and it works. Don't say I told you so!

That side trip was more valuable to the group than your need to be right. The group had to go through the experience to see how to get where they needed to go. Once they decide what they need, they believe in it because they decided. That's medicine more powerful than any you can administer.

Know your art, be confident, and be flexible.
Any rigidity in your character will be blown away in the first five minutes, so you might as well go in loose!

I have talked a lot about planning and preparing and its importance. That's still valid. However, being a Person-Centred Manager is rather like being in quantum physics these days. You must consider the possibility that the real nature of the universe is one of chaos. But even in chaotic systems, the physicists tell us, the random and unpredictable movements never exceed finite boundaries.

Your plan, your techniques, your knowledge and your agenda are the boundaries. The people, their personalities, the problem and you are the random and unpredictable movements. Confidence and intelligent flexibility are your lifelines.

Warning! Ambience may impair your ability to be creative. If creativity is an important element of the session:

- Get the group members as far away from their offices as you can, mentally and physically.

- Provide a relaxed atmosphere.

- Turn off the left brain by doing something that disorients it: something wild, fast, up-side-down, inside-out, too slow or too fast. Get them laughing. Pop them out of their normal world and normal way of doing business. Turn on the music, get out the crayons.

Preserve the integrity of the group and every individual.
I have avoided the use of 'should' and 'must' and 'never' in this book because I don't like other people's fingers shaking in our faces...but here is an exception: you must never violate the integrity of the group or anyone in it.

Never
- Admonish a participant or the group

- Insult the organisation or anyone in it

- Insult an outside organisation or person

- Argue with a participant

- Ignore a participant

- Endorse gossip

- Support deprecating remarks

- Take sides on an issue

- Endorse some participants and not others

- Disapprove of an action, comment, or behaviour (watch body language)

Do
- Take diversity training

- Welcome all feedback from participants

- Allow all comments, even the 'stupid' ones

Learn to laugh at yourself.
The trait that I've received more compliments on than any other, from people who have attended our sessions, is the ability to hold up under fire. If I didn't have this ability, I wouldn't do it. The key was learning to laugh at myself. It wasn't an inborn trait for me, I actually had to force myself to

do it during my early Person-Centred sessions.

Learn to recognise signs of when a good laugh is in order: things like 1) wanting to rip someone's lips off, 2) defending what you are doing, or 3) qualifying your right to say what you are saying.

Force yourself to think "Heaven forbid, I'm not perfect!" and laugh. Laughter depersonalises the comment or situation so that you can manage it, which is what you were hired to do.

Two camps, no movement.
All occupational groups have their own nightmares, those they sleep through and those they live through. The nightmare of the Person-Centred Manager is to have the group stake out two camps, hashing and re-hashing the issue, getting nowhere. Most Person-Centred Managers will have this kind of nightmare. There's good news from the front: You can do something about it!

When a group cannot reach consensus, when two camps have been posted, there's a reason, a valid reason, behind the disagreement. I've found that usually the argument is over one thing, but the actual disagreement lies below the topic being argued. It is your job to root it out.

The Go Around technique works to explore the reasons for the disagreement (later in this chapter. In **Go Around**, everyone hears all facets of the issue. Each member listens to what the others think, thus all important factors come forward. In addition, this technique is effective for refocusing a discussion that may have become heated, confrontational and, possibly, personalised.

When everyone is given the opportunity to contribute, 'air time' and pressure is removed from the more vocal members of each camp. The viewpoints are depersonalised. The very fact that Go Around takes a while can help cool down participants.

Through this technique, you will get a feel for how many

people are in each camp, but do not use this for a majority vote. By knowing where participants stand on the issue, you can narrow your focus and surface the real cause of the disagreement. Listen like a detective to what each side is saying. Listen objectively, looking for facts, trends and commonalties.

At the end of the Go Around, summarise what you believe to be the essence of the problem. Ask the group how the issue can be dealt with. Keep them focused on the isolated issues you have found and keep them in problem solving mode. Usually once you work through this process, the group will discover the real nature of the disagreement.

It is important that you stick with the issue (if it is an important one) until it is resolved. It may not be simple, quick and conflict-free, but if you take them to the depths, the reason for disagreement will be found and the problem solved.

Usually, **lack of consensus results from a lack of common understanding.**

If consensus can't be reached, you may have to ask one camp or the other to live with the decision or you may request that the group table it for later. DO get closure on the issue. DO NOT brush it away or try to avoid the inherent conflict. If you must ask one camp to concede, either permanently or for now, be sure and get them to agree to the concession. You can't order them to do it. Your goal is to get spoken closure agreement, so that the issue isn't left hanging open where the group will continue to stumble over it.

A True Story

In my most memorable Two Camp Experience, I took them through Go Around, did my detective work and finally gave up. In desperation, I asked the last holdout if he could just live with the decision of the rest of the group and trust them. That's when the real problem came out. He said: "it is not that I don't trust this group, I don't trust management, and I think that if this group produces this information, it'll be used to all of our detriment." Guess what? The rest of the group agreed completely with his sentiment. The group had another view of how they could publish and use the information in a way to disarm its negative effect. As soon as they worked out those details, all were in agreement.

Consensus

Here are some guidelines for helping the group to achieve consensus.

- Help group members to avoid arguing for their own position. If needed, help them present it logically, but be prepared to intervene.

- Look for win-win alternatives. As the Person-Centred Manager, you are working for collaboration and co-operation, not competition where there are winners and losers.

- If agreement seems to come too quickly, be suspicious. Some people change to avoid conflict. Explore the reasons. Be sure everyone accepts the solution for similar or complementary reasons.

- Avoid conflict reducing techniques such as majority vote, coin flips, and bargaining. Differences of opinion are natural and expected. They increase the group's decision-making ability by providing a greater range of information and opinions. As the Person-Centred Manager, you have techniques to use for the group to come to consensus, such as the Nominal Group Technique or Multi-Voting.

Putting it all together.

By now you may be absolutely overwhelmed by all of the things a Person-Centred Manager must do. Don't worry, remember that this book is a compilation of what I have learned in hundreds of hours of managing sessions. The most valuable tips came from mistakes I made. To help you keep on track, as you integrate and add to your knowledge, you might use questions such as these during breaks and between sessions to evaluate your own progress.

- Am I producing the products?

- Am I sticking to the agenda?

- Is everyone participating?

- Is there any dysfunctional behaviour?

- Do they need a break or change-of-pace activity?

- Is anyone frustrated?

- Can everyone see what the group is doing?

- Am I being objective?

Intervention.

In an intervention, the Person-Centred Manager's role is changed from that of a passive observer to that of an active participant. This highlights the distinction between observation and intervention. A Person-Centred Manager observes to determine if intervention is needed. Intervention is deliberate breaking into the task and process of the group and should be done only after observation has occurred. Lacking observation, the Person-Centred Manager has no valid reason for intervening. Interventions are primarily focused on the process of group operation.

The Person-Centred Manager has the unique role of ensuring that the meeting remains organised and productive. For that reason, the Person-Centred Manager must, in addition to his or her other capabilities, acquire an ability to intervene during a meeting when it becomes apparent that members need assistance.

Intervention strategies are a particularly sensitive area. It is important to remember that the Person-Centred Manager usually isn't a member of the group. The Person-Centred Manager is, or acts as the third party, the neutral observer possessing the interpersonal skills to foster more harmonious relationships.

When to intervene?

1. Immediately — because the consequences of not intervening

155

would have some serious impact on the group.

2. At the first opportunity (end of a topic discussion or at some change in the task activity). The Person-Centred Manager may choose to allow small conceptual or process issues to go uncorrected to see how and when anyone handles the issue or to allow the group to learn from its own behaviours.

3. At some later time because the activity will occur again and provide a better opportunity for the group to accept intervention.

Why intervene?

There are three types of intervention, each serving a different purpose:

1. Procedural intervention is used to clear up confusion concerning process improvement procedures — what to do or how to do it.

2. Conceptual intervention is used when the Person-Centred Manager observes confusion or lack of understanding concerning a major concept, technique, or problem solving tool. It is frequently instructional in nature.

3. Process intervention is used to focus attention on some interpersonal or group dynamic obstacle which will seriously affect the outcome of the group's efforts. It seeks to identify, solve, and remove the obstacle.

Where should the Person-Centred Manager intervene?

Most interventions occur in the meeting room. Interventions made outside the meeting normally involve issues or problems best handled with a specific member of the group. For example, a personality clash between members or continued disruptive behaviour by a group member would best be handled outside of the meeting.

How might the Person-Centred Manager intervene?

This is the most difficult question to answer because it is an intricate aspect of the Person-Centred Manager's style and everyday behaviour. The question breaks down into whether the Person-Centred Manager will simply tell or, through questioning, help the group discover the problem.

Each question needs to be thoughtfully considered before intervening. Using a casual and unplanned intervention strategy is opening the door to potentially adverse consequences for both yourself and the group. Frequent interventions may lead to dependence on the Person-Centred Manager, lessening the group's ability to develop competence and independence.

An overly aggressive Person-Centred Manager can adversely affect group relationships if he or she intervenes or interrupts too often. Frequent interventions may be perceived as undermining the responsibility and authority of the group. On the other hand, a timid Person-Centred Manager will miss critical opportunities for intervention that could enhance group process and relationships.

Several principles that guide good Person-Centred Management sessions and answer the 'when to intervene question' include:

1. Group cohesiveness and morale are highly desirable.

2. A positive relationship between the leader of the group and members of the group is important.

3. A good Person-Centred Manager is a skilled listener, speaking only when absolutely necessary or when responding to a question.

4. Interventions during meetings will be positively viewed by members if they're perceived as necessary, timely and productive.

When you design a session, you select the techniques you think will work for the specific agenda items. Be prepared for the unexpected! Don't hesitate to create a new technique on the spot.

Don't hesitate to tap into the group's ideas. Ask them to help. Enlist them as your allies. If they invent a technique, it becomes their technique and they love it. Never forget the basic rule: **People support what they help to create.**

Go Around

A technique to encourage contribution toward group decision making. The Person-Centred Manager begins at one end of the table. Each person is given the chance to say how he or she views the issue, state their idea, etc. If a person chooses to say nothing in this round, he or she says "pass."

Each person should be satisfied that he or she had a chance to influence the decision and declare a willingness or unwillingness to support it.

The term **consensus** means that support is derived from each person feeling heard and understood. This technique helps build and maintain group cohesiveness.

Please State Your Needs

A technique to gain clarity and honesty.

Simply ask the person or ask the group (by using the Go Around technique) to please state their needs. Here's an example: The Person-Centred Manager senses the group needs a break even though it is not scheduled and they would say, "Please state your needs. I need to know if you feel a short break is appropriate."

The Constructive Response

A technique used to create a product from breakout groups' individual products. This is a very simple and very effective technique used by Person-Centred Managers.

Basic Version: Using the Go Around technique, have each person:

1. Say for example what they like about the idea or proposal under consideration.

2. Next, ask each person to state their concerns.

3. Assist and encourage people to find ways to overcome the concerns.

Alternative Version

This technique is especially valuable when a Person-Centred Manager has a large group and must break them into smaller groups. When each team brings its proposal or solution back to the whole group, use the Constructive Response to examine each group's proposal. On the easel or chalkboard, list the likes and list the concerns with each group's proposal. Place them with that proposal on the wall or hang them together using easels.

When this is completed, the Person-Centred Manager begins the process of having the group come up with the final product. One of two things generally happens:

1. The group combines the likes from each sub-group and there is no further need for the concerns lists.

2. The group combines all the likes from each sub-group and uses the concerns list as a check to make sure the group product has avoided anything that has caused concern to someone. If there is a concern, the group talks it out.

Take Five

A technique to accommodate different thinking styles or preferences and help discussions begin quickly and on-track.

Individuals have preferences in how they think and make decisions. Some people are extroverts, and prefer thinking out loud. Introverts prefer thinking silently. The Take Five technique guarantees those with an introverted thinking style the time (five minutes or less) and silence they need for organising their thoughts. Understanding others without trying to alter or judge their behaviour is an ability in itself. Allowing for differences maximises each person's ability to contribute.

After you begin the session by stating the purpose for bringing the participants together, acknowledge the differing preferences or styles that people will be using during the session. Tell them you will use a technique that will accommodate their different thinking styles.

When assigning members to breakout groups, suggest each

person take a few minutes (or five) to organise their thoughts and ideas. They can make a written list if they wish. You may ask participants to do this before the session begins and bring their notes. After this brief quiet period, the group then begins discussion. This procedure permits those who need it, quiet time to organise their thoughts without distraction.

It is always advisable to provide advance information about a meeting. Extroverts do not need it and probably won't even read it, but introverts DO and WILL.

Put It In The Hangar
A technique to avoid side-tracks. During the session, it is easy for groups to get off the issue, or get side-tracked by other issues, ideas or even people. Although such issues or ideas may later be determined to be relevant, their relevance is unclear at the moment.

To capture these, label a piece of flip chart paper as The Hangar. Whenever a side issue or idea emerges, list it there. These issues can be addressed at a later time.

This technique captures all ideas and issues during a session and acknowledges the contribution or participation of each member, even if their idea or issue is not the primary one under consideration.

Brainstorming
A technique to generate ideas quickly. Everyone is familiar with brainstorming.

The conceptual rules are:

- No criticism or evaluation

- Be unconventional

- Aim for quantity

- Hitchhike on other ideas

The practical rules are:

- Everyone contributes

- One idea per turn

- You may pass

Brainstorming can be modified and effectively used in certain situations which require the fast generation of ideas from a group. In addition, varying the technique introduces a new way of brainstorming and of enjoying the unconventionality of these modifications.

Alternative #1

1. A time limit is set.

2. Each participant works alone.

3. Each participant puts his or her ideas on a large self-sticking note. Only one idea per note is allowed.

4. Each idea is posted to a wall, board, or easel.

5. At the end of the time period, the group uses grouping techniques, like the Affinity Diagram (described later in this chapter) to combine ideas.

Alternative #2

Same rules as above except:

1. Instead of self-sticking notes, each participant uses index cards. Again only one idea per card is allowed.

2. As they finish each card, participants say the idea out loud and throw the card into the middle of the group. The Person-Centred Manager collects them as they're being thrown.

The alternatives have very real advantages for certain situations.

1. They take away judgement and censorship.

2. Pressure to perform is removed.

3. The volume of ideas generated increases.

Because brainstorming produces a lot of ideas without filtering, be sure you know what to do next with the product of the brainstorm and make sure that the participants know what is going to happen as well.

Nominal Group Technique (NGT)
A technique which combines brainstorming and the benefits of individual thought. NGT is a technique used to:

1. Identify processes.

2. Develop a process statement.

3. List the causes that reduce process effectiveness.

4. Prepare for data collection.

5. Identify solutions that improve processes.

NGT reduces the tendency of groups to evaluate ideas when they're presented.

NGT is a method of drawing out as many ideas as possible and then reducing the field of ideas to just a few.

The goal of NGT is to be as expansive with ideas as possible and then to select the most workable ideas the group can use to go on to the next step in the process.

The Person-Centred Manager guides the group through the NGT steps:

1. Group members silently generate a list of ideas on paper.

2. All ideas are recorded on a large sheet of paper. Once group members appear to have finished listing their ideas silently, the Person-Centred Manager will begin by having the member to the immediate right or left give the first idea on his or her list. The Person-Centred Manager will write the idea, exactly as expressed, on the paper. Initials of the individual giving the idea may

be placed on the sheet by his or her idea if further clarification may be needed. Otherwise, do not pin ideas to people. Let ideas become group ideas.

Items should be numbered and written so that they may be easily read by the entire group. When an idea is recorded, it shouldn't be explained or clarified, merely posted. This process continues with each member giving one idea per turn, until all of the members' ideas are exhausted.

3. Ideas are discussed for clarification. Once all the ideas have been listed, the Person-Centred Manager will go around the group again and ask each member in turn if there are any items on the list which are not understood or which need to be clarified.

4. Once all items have been clarified and are understood, the group participates in an anonymous vote on the ideas.

The voting is accomplished on secret ballots, which are then passed to a group member to be read and recorded. After tabulation, the group can easily see which of the items is of greatest interest to the group. The natural by-product of this step is that the group's attention is directed to the items that received the largest number of votes. If votes are evenly distributed, that fact captures the group's attention. The purpose of this step is to determine where group interest lies. Remember that all items listed, no matter how few votes they may have received, remain candidates for future consideration until the group decides otherwise.

5. The group discusses remaining items, if necessary. At this point, all group members should understand what is meant by each item on the list. If a member has strong feelings about an item that was not selected, the member should explain to the group why he or she feels so strongly. If the individual feels strongly that the item should be placed on the selected list, place it there.

6. When all discussion has been exhausted, the group ranks items selected through a weighted voting process. Once again, each member will cast an anonymous paper ballot, but this time each vote will be weighted on the basis of the total number of items included in the vote. For example, if five items are included in the vote, each

member will give five votes to the item that is most important, four votes to the second most important item, and so on.

Multi-Voting

A technique to reduce the number of ideas to a manageable size. The objective in Multi-Voting is to reduce the number of ideas, not to arrive at a final choice. It can be used when brainstorming has generated too many items to be addressed at one time.

1. Group members vote for as many ideas from the list as they wish, but may cast only one vote for each item.

2. The list is trimmed by one-half, with those ideas having the fewest votes dropped.

3. Each member votes for half of the remaining ideas.

4. The voting process continues until the predetermined number of ideas is reached.

Guided Discussion

A technique used to guide group discussion. It can be built-in when you design the session. You may need to use it unexpectedly when the group raises an issue that is new or controversial and a time-out from what they are doing to discuss the issue is necessary. This technique allows for specific subjects to be discussed in a specified amount of time.

1. Prepare an open-ended question for each of the topic areas to be discussed.

2. Give about two minutes of introductory background information and briefly mention each topic or issue that will be covered during the discussion. State the amount of time that will be allowed for each topic or issue.

3. Ask the question you prepared for the first topic.

4. Saying nothing, observe the process intently. Do not become involved in the content. The Person-Centred Manager guides the discussion but can't become part of the discussion.

5. Intervene quickly, but only when needed, to assist the process.

6. Monitor the time and move to the next topic using a transition statement.

7. Ask the question for the second topic.

8. If discussion digresses from the topic, bring it back on track without stifling additional ideas. Use The Hangar technique if appropriate.

9. After discussing all topics, give a quick summary of the ideas presented and decisions made. Express appreciation for the group's participation.

Mediating Conflict between Two People in a Group Environment:

A Person-Centred Manager can help group members resolve conflicts which can improve interpersonal relationships. Unresolved conflicts negatively affect group productivity and relationships. The following process can be used with the entire group present.

1. Get agreement from the members in conflict and from the group to proceed. You may wish to explain that this is a process that can be used whenever conflict arises and the advantage of having a third party guide the conflict resolution process.

2. The two people in conflict sit facing each other. The Person-Centred Manager is seated so that he or she can see their faces clearly.

3. The PCM asks one person to explain what the conflict is about and how he or she feels. The second person listens and is then asked to paraphrase what was said. Next, the second person states what he or she thinks the problem is about and his or her feelings. The first person listens, then is asked to paraphrase what was said.

4. In the second round, the first person states the desired outcome. The second listens, then paraphrases. Then, the second person states the desired outcome. His or her words are then paraphrased by the first person.

5. The process of stating, listening, and paraphrasing is

continued. The goal is to clarify the issues, hear the desired outcomes, and find a solution. When consensus is reached and both agree to a solution, the process is complete.

6. The entire group evaluates how the mediation process worked. First, the Person-Centred Manager asks the two participants how it felt and what steps of the process helped. Then, other group members are asked to state their observations. Finally, the group discusses how the mediated process could be used in the future.

The Affinity Diagram
A technique to organise facts or issues into groups or clusters. This technique is useful if the problem or issue is highly complex and needs the total involvement of the group.

First, present the problem or issue to the group. Then do Brainstorming. Set a time limit like seven minutes. Ask members to silently generate as many ideas as possible. Have them place each idea on a separate self-sticking note. Give members big markers so the word or phrases they write can be read easily.

When the time is up, place all self-sticking notes on a wall. Ask group members to organise them into groups or clusters that appear to have some sort of relationship. As the groups or clusters are developed, each begins to have a closer relationship with the issues or facts placed with them. Each member is free to change the self-sticking notes. When it appears the group members have reached consensus and are satisfied with the relationships, the information can then be used to continue work on the issue or problem.

This technique works very well for a comprehensive agenda item like developing organisational values, as well as for a very specific agenda item like defining all the tasks needed to complete a work activity.

This technique is not for problems or issues requiring immediate solution.

Fish Bowl

A dramatic and 'last resort' technique used to break an impasse in discussion when closure is required. It isn't unusual, when bringing individual group products together, that the groups cannot agree. Quite frequently, they end up doubling the number of ideas instead of getting to closure. Do not be surprised when you try to bring a group to closure and a group member develops a new idea and interrupts what is going on to present it because he or she is so enthusiastic about it.

You will probably be using The Constructive Response and Go Around to combine group ideas. What you may see happening instead is an opening of discussion and more idea creation. When you find yourself feeling out of control and not knowing what to do to bring structure back to this process, you will know this is the time to yell 'Fish Bowl!'

1. Call a 10 minute time out. Tell members of each group to select a representative who is empowered to make decisions for the group.

2. Advise the group that, on their return to the room, they will find chairs in the middle of the room for each group's representative. There will also be one additional chair. All other group members will sit in the outer circle of chairs. Final directions will be given at that time. Then have all group members leave the room.

3. Configure the room, placing the representatives' chairs and one additional chair within the inner circle. With the rest of the chairs, form a semi-circle around the inner circle, for the rest of the participants.

4. Begin the Fish Bowl by stating that representatives will reach a consensus on the issue in twenty minutes. They'll speak with sufficient volume to be heard by the entire group. No communication will be permitted between the inner and outer circles. Anyone wishing to address the representatives in the inner circle will be granted one minute to sit in the extra chair and state his or her position to the representatives.

5. The Person-Centred Manager steps back as the inner circle of representatives work towards consensus.

6. The Person-Centred Manager must intervene if the

guidelines are not followed. Intervention is crucial to ensure that no communication occurs between the circles. Failure to intervene returns the group to its starting point with everyone talking or arguing.

7. When consensus is reached, thank the group and move on to the next agenda item.

The first time you do this you will probably feel afraid. Mask your fear. You must be in complete control. Usually it will not be a problem for you because you will feel so irritated at what is going on in the group you will want to take control! That is your clue to yell Fish Bowl!

Group Evaluation
There will be times when you work with groups who need to evaluate themselves. The information will help you and the group to modify activities, resolve conflicts, make better use of time, or solve problems differently. There are a variety of ways to do this.

One simple way is to decide which areas would benefit from evaluation. The following is a list of commonly used categories:

- Goals

- Commitment

- Procedures and Guidelines

- Roles

- Participation

- Trust

- Conflict

- Hidden Agendas

- Timing

- Level of interest

- Synergy

- Feelings

- Problem solving methods

- Person-Centred Management (yes, ask how you are doing also!)

Develop a rating scale for each area. I suggest a rating scale of one to five to keep it simple. Have one as the low end and five as the high end. For each end, give an appropriate description so everyone understands what is being asked. The following are examples to help you design your own:

Person-Centred Management
1 2 3 4 5
Inappropriate amount of direction --- Just the right amount direction

Trust
1 2 3 4 5
Low level of trust --- High level of trust

The rating scale evaluation can be used for a group that has been working together for some time.

It can also be used as a diagnostic tool for a Person-Centred Management session designed to improve the teamwork of the participants. Before the session, the questionnaire can be given to the participants. Ask them to complete the evaluation anonymously. Explain to them that this information will be used to discuss how to improve the group's working together.

Another evaluation format is a list of questions that allows each person to state their thoughts about each question. This method takes longer to do and will require time to compile the results. However, it provides more in-depth information than the rating scale.

The following is an example:

How well are we working together?

1. How did you feel when you first formed this group (or team)?

2. How do you feel now?

3. Which of the group's (or team's) goals do you think you have achieved?

4. What unresolved conflicts do you think this group (or team) needs to address?

5. What prevents you from being more committed, interested or participate more?

6. How can the Person-Centred Manager help your group (or team) move forward?

7. Does your group (or team) need any additional ground rules or procedures?

8. What is not happening that, if it did happen, would make your group (or team) more successful?

9. What are the three best things about your group (or team)?

10. What is the one thing you would like to see happen that you think is impossible for your group (or team)?

Conclusion

It is obvious that the key issue in today's global **business** environment is **staff retention**. Without staff, **integrated** well into the company and contributing their maximum **effort**, success is short-term. Problems, particularly **with personnel**, have knock-on effects causing problems with training, planning and strategic decision-making.

It makes sense therefore to consider carefully the reasons why people leave companies and why they stay. When set in a global context this becomes even more complex and so a multi-cultural approach has to be put in place. This, however, has to be done, not just with company profits in mind, but with the interests of the individual who comprises this valuable workforce carefully addressed. Respect for people **has to be genuine** and not just another human resources exercise designed as a cosmetic gloss on driving human endeavour further.

It means taking time to listen to people, considering their needs as individuals and matching them with work which will gratify them and satisfy their need to feel part of a worthwhile organisation. In a multicultural environment this includes understanding social mores and traditions and working to accommodate them. Teaching immigrants our ways/mores/traditions/helps them to adapt not just socially but also in the practicalities of business. In order for this to occur, especially in Ireland as it is a relatively newly developed country, we need to develop managers to be strong leaders, showing respect for everyone as individuals and not as cogs in a wheel which rolls for profit only.

What does it mean in the context of organisations? We have learned that job dissatisfaction results from the person not being honestly respected, so job satisfaction will be generated by a recognition of this very basic need. This is the key to any cultural diversity programme as witnessed throughout the developed world.

I believe that groups of people working together create more than individuals working alone. We empower each other. Everyone, in their heart, desires to work in harmony with each other.

I hope my beliefs have come alive for you through this book. Once people start to open to the possibility that groups of people, working together, can accomplish more than they ever dreamed possible, dramatic breakthroughs are made and the problem of staff retention is constructively addressed in the long term for the good of everyone.

Bibliography

Ames, Helen Wattley, *Spain is different* Yarmouth (Maine): Intercultural Press, 1992

Ardagh, John *Ireland & the Irish*. 1990

Ardagh, John *Germany and the Germans*. London, Penguin 1990.

Ardagh, John *France in the 1980s: The Definitive Book,* Harmondsworth: Penguin 1982

Ardagh, John *France Today* Penguin London 1987
Bedian, A.G., Ferris, G. R., & Kacmar, K.M. (1994). *Age, tenure, and job satisfaction: A tale of two perspectives*. Journal of Vocational Behaviour, 40, 33-48.

Becker, H.S . (1960). *Notes on the concept of commitment*. American Journal of Sociology, 66, 32-40.

Becker, T.E., & Billings, R.s (1993). *Profiles of commitment: An empirical test*. Journal of Organisational Behaviour, 14, 177-190.

Bond Michael Harris *The Psychology of the Chinese People*. Oxford University Press 1986

Caldwell, D.F., Chatman, J.A., & O'Reilly,C.A. (1990). *Building organisational commitment: A multiform study*. Journal of Occupational Psychology, 63, 245-261.

Carnevale, A.P., & Stone, S.C. (1995). *The American mosaic: An in-depth report on the future of diversity at work*. New York: McGraw-Hill.

Carsten,J.M.,& Spector, P.E. (1987). *Unemployment, job satisfaction, and employee turnover: A meta-analytic test of the Murchinsky model*. Journal of Applied Psychology, 72, 374-381.

Cartwright, D. (1970). *The nature of group cohesiveness*. In D. Cartwright & A. Zander (Eds.), Group dynamics: research and theory (3rd ed., pp.

91-109). New York: Harper &Row.

"Cross-border investment is high."(1993, September 15). Chemical Week, P.5).

Dalton, D.R., & Todor, W.D. (1993) . *Turnover, transfer, absenteeism: An interdependent perspective.* Journal of Management, 19, 193-219.

Cox, T.C., Jr. (1994). *Cultural diversity in organisations.* San Francisco: Berrett-Kohler.

Curry, J.P., Wakefield, D.S., Price, J.L., & Mueller, C.W. (1986). *On the causal ordering of job satisfaction and organisational commitment.* Academy of management Journal, 29, 8467-858.

DeCieri, H., & Dowling, P.J. (1995). *Cross-cultural issues in organisational behaviour.* In C.L. Cooper & D.M. Rousseau (Eds), Trends in organisational behaviour (Vol.2, pp. 127-145). New York: John Wiley & Sons.

Dunham, R.B., Grube, J.A., & Castaneda, M.B. (1994). *Organisational commitment: The utility of an integrative definition.* Journal of Applied Psychology, 79, 370-380.

Earley, P.C., & Singh, H. (1995). *International and inter-cultural management research: What's next?* Academy of Management Journal, 38, 327-340.

A Survey of multinationals, (1993), March 27). The Economist, p.6.

Eichar, D.M., Brady, E.M., & Fortinsky, R.H. (1991). *The job satisfaction of older workers.* Journal of Organisational Behaviour, 12, 609-620.

Flower Raymond & Falassi Alessandro *Culture Shock* (series).

Forsyth, D.R. (1992) . *An introduction to group dynamics,* (2nd ed.). Monterey, CA : Brooks/Cole.

Gutek, B.A., & Winter, S.J. (1992). *Consistency of job satisfaction across situations: Fact or framing artifact?* Journal of Vocational Behaviour, 41, 61-78.

Hackett, R.D., Boycio, P.,& Hausdorf, P.A. (1995). *Further assessments of Meyer and Allen's (1991) three-component model of organisational commitment.* Journal of applied psychology, 79, 15-23.

Hall Kevan *Effective Cross Cultural Meetings.*

Hampden-Turner Charles *The Seven Cultures of Capitalism.*1994

Herzberg, F. (1966). *Work and the nature of man.* Cleveland: World.

Hill Richard *We Europeans.*

Hise, P. (1994) *The motivational employee satisfaction questionnaire.* Inc., pp. 73-75.

Hofstede, G. (1980). *Culture's consequences: International differences in work related values.* Beverly Hills, CA: Sage.

Hofstede Geert *Software of the Mind.*

Hulin,C.L. (1991). *Adaption, persistence, and commitment in organisations.* In M.D. Dunnette & L. M. Hough (Eds), Handbook of industrial and organisational psychology (2nd ed., Vol. 2, pp. 445-506). Palo Alto, CA: Consulting Psychologists Press.

Huntington, S.P. (1993, summer). *The clash of civilisations.* Foreign Affairs, pp. 22-49.Janssens, M. (1995). *Intercultural interaction: A burden on international managers?* Journal of Organisational Behaviour, 16, 155-167.

Iaffaldano, M.T., & Murchinsky, P.M. (1985). *Job satisfaction and job performance: A meta-analysis.* Psychological Bulletin, 97, 251-273.

Kenna Peggy & Lacy Sondra *Business* (series) e.g. Business Japan

Lambert, S.L. (1991). *The combined effect of job and family characteristics on the job satisfaction, job involvement , and intrinsic motivation of men and women workers.* Journal of Organisational behaviour, 12, 341-363.

Landy, F.J. (1985) *Psychology of work behaviour* (3rd ed.). Homewood, IL:

Dorsey.

Lee, T.W., Ashford, S.J., Walsh, J.P., & Mowday, R.T. (1992). *Commitment propensity, organisational commitment, and voluntary turnover: A longitudinal study of organisational entry processes.* Journal of Management, 18, 15-32.

Lewis Richard *When Cultures Collide.*

Locke, E.A. (1976). *The nature and causes of job satisfaction.* In M.D. Dunnette (Ed.), Handbook of industrial and organisational psychology (pp. 1297-1350) . Chicago: Rand McNally.

Locke, E.A. (1984). *Job satisfaction.* In M. Gruenberg & T. Wall (Eds), Social psychology and organisational behaviour (pp. 93- 117). London: Wiley.

Lodge, G.C. (1995). *Managing globalisation in the age of interdependence.* San Diego, CA: Pfeffer.

Long,S.(1984). *Early integration in groups: "A group to join and a group to create."* Human Relations, 37,311-322.

McGuire, W.J. (1985). *Attitudes and attitude change.* In G. Lindzey & E. Aronson (Eds.) Handbook of social psychology (3rd ed., Vol. 2, pp. 233-346). New York: Random House.

Machungaws, P.D., & Schmitt, N. (1983). *Work motivation in a developing country.* Journal of Applied Psychology, 68, 31-42.

Mathiew, J.E., & Zajoc, D.M. (1990). *A review and meta-analysis of the antecedents, correlates, and consequences of commitment.* Psychological Bulletin, 108, 171-194.

Meyer, J.P., & Allen, N.J. (1991). *A three-component conceptualisation of organisational commitment.* Human Resource Management Review, 1, 61-89.

Mobley, W.H., Horner S.O., & Hollingsworth, A.T. (1978). *An evaluation of precursors of hospital employee turnover.* Journal of Applied Psychology, 63, 408-414.

Murray Bosrock Mary *Put your best foot forward Europe.*
Corbett James *Through French Windows.* University of Michigan Press.

Ogbonna, E. (1993). *Managing organisational culture: Fantasy or reality?* Human resource Management Journal, 3(2), 42-54.

Page, N.R., & Wiseman, R.L (1993). *Supervisory behaviour and worker satisfaction in the United States, Mexico and Spain.* Journal of Business communication, 30, 161-180.

Porter, L.W., & Steers, R.M., (1973). *Organisational work and personal factors in employee turnover and absenteeism.* Psychological Bulletin, 80, 151-176.

Quarstein,V.A., McAfee, R.b.,&Glassman, M. (1992). *The situational occurrences theory of Job Satisfaction.* Human relations, 45, 859-873.

Randall, D.M. (1990). *The consequences of organisational commitment: A methodological investigation.* Journal of Organisational Behaviour, 11, 361-378.

Randall, D.M., Fedor D.P., & Longenecker, C.O. (1990). *The behavioural expression of organisational commitment.* Journal of Vocational Behaviour, 36, 210-224.

Reichers, A.E. (1985). *A review and reconceptualisation of organisational commitment.* Academy of management Review, 10, 465-476.

Romzek, B.S. (1989). *Personal consequences of employee commitment.* Academy of Management Journal, 39, 641-661.

Ronen, S. (1986). *Comparative multinational management.* New York: Wiley.

Seybolt, Peter J., *Through Chinese Eyes* CITE Books.

Shaw, M.E. (1981). *Group dynamics: The dynamics of small group behaviour* (3rd ed.). new York: McGraw-Hill.
Weaver, C.N. (1980). *Job satisfaction in the United States in the 1970s.* Journal of Applied Psychology, 65, 364-367.

Somers, M.J. (1995). *Organisational commitment, turnover and absenteeism: An examination of direct and interaction effects.* Journal of organisational behaviour, 16, 49-58.

Staw, B.M., & Ross, J. (1995). *Stability in the midst of change: A dispositional approach to job attitudes.* Journal of Applied Psychology, 70, 56-77.

Terrill Ross – *The Australians.* New York Simon & Schuster 1987.

Tett, R.P., & Meyer, J.P. (1993). *Job satisfaction, organisational commitment, turnover intention, and turnover: Path analyses based on meta-analytic findings.* Personnel Psychology, 46, 259-293.

Trompenaars Fons., *Riding the Waves of Culture.* 1995

Vancouver, J.B., Milsap, R.E., & Peters, P.A. (1994). *Multilevel analysis of organisational goal congruence.* Journal of Applied Psychology, 79, 666-679.

Vandenberg, R.J., & Lance, C.E. (1992). *Examining the causal order of job satisfaction and organisational commitment.* Journal of Management, 18, 153-167.

Wenzhong, Hu & Grove Cornelius L Intercultural Press, Inc 1991

Whitener, E. M., & Waltz, P.M. (1993). *Exchange theory determinants of affective and continuance commitment and turnover.* Journal of Vocational Behaviour, 42, 265-281.

Index